This book is due on the last date stamped below.
Failure to return books on the date due may result
in assessment of overdue fees.

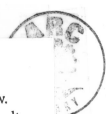

This Brief Tragedy

UNRAVELING THE TODD-DICKINSON AFFAIR

JOHN EVANGELIST WALSH

GROVE WEIDENFELD

NEW YORK

Published by Grove Weidenfeld
A division of Grove Press, Inc.
841 Broadway
New York, New York 10003–4793

Published in Canada by General Publishing Company, Ltd.

Library of Congress Cataloging-in-Publication Data

Walsh, John Evangelist, 1927–
This brief tragedy : unraveling the Todd-Dickinson affair / John
Evangelist Walsh. — 1st ed.
p.   cm.
Includes bibliographical references and index.
ISBN 0-8021-1119-X
1. Dickinson, Emily, 1830–1886—Biography—Family.   2. Dickinson,
Austin, d. 1895—Relations with women.   3. Todd, Mabel Loomis,
1856–1932—Relations with men.   4. Scandals—Massachusetts—
Amherst—History—19th century.   5. Poets, American—19th
century—Biography—Family.   6. Amherst (Mass.)—Biography.
I. Title.
PS1541.Z5W27   1991
811'.4—dc20
[B]   91-10945
                                                              CIP

Manufactured in the United States of America

Printed on acid-free paper

Designed by Irving Perkins Associates

First Edition 1991

1   3   5   7   9   10   8   6   4   2

DEDICATED

In all affection, still,
to those several scholars,
living and dead,
with whom I have in the
following pages
so roundly disagreed.
If I should prove wrong
I pray their forgiveness.
If I should prove right
I pray all to forgive them.

Acknowledgments

For incisive readings of the manuscript, helping to sharpen and refine the presentation, I am grateful to Timothy A. Walsh, University of Wisconsin; John C. Walsh, George Mason University; and Walt Bode, Grove Weidenfeld. Also, for research assistance, I am indebted to Ann A. Walsh, and for helpful comment to Matthew O. Walsh.

Permission to quote from specific sources, published and unpublished, is hereby acknowledged:

Yale University Library for the journals, diaries, and letters of Mabel Loomis Todd and for the diaries and letters of Austin Dickinson; same for extracts from various court papers in the Todd-Dickinson lawsuit;

Amherst College Library, by permission of the Trustees of Amherst College, for an unpublished letter of Susan Dickinson;

Houghton Library, Harvard University, for the Dickinson family letters.

The Belknap Press of Harvard University, *The Letters of Emily Dickinson*, ed. T. H. Johnson, copyright © 1958, 1986; same for *The Poems of Emily Dickinson*, ed. T. H. Johnson, copyright © 1951, 1955, 1979, 1983, with permission of the Trustees of Amherst College.

Contents

"Generally I claim (not arrogantly, but with firmness) the merit of rectification applied to absolute errors, or to injudicious limitations of the truth."

—De Quincey

This
Brief Tragedy

UNRAVELING THE
TODD-DICKINSON
AFFAIR

Prologue: *Gib's Room*

FOR ITS PECULIAR POWER of literary fascination, joined to elemental human drama, the tree-studded Dickinson enclave in Amherst, Massachusetts, can have few equals. During more than a century and a half its two stately homes, standing some sixty yards apart, have risen impressively behind a double barrier of fence and hedge. Separated only by a tall, leafy grove—through the grove still runs the original, moss-grown pathway linking the two houses— together they continue to hold center stage in Emily's supremely compelling story. Yet the careers of these two distinguished houses in later times have not been at all alike.

Emily's house, a sturdy but graceful brick structure called the Mansion or the Homestead, eventually became the property of Amherst College, and its doors have long been open to literary pilgrims. Her brother Austin's house, called the Evergreens and built entirely of wood, has always remained in private hands, firmly beyond the possibility of inspection except by an occasional few. My own visit was the unexpected result of a spur-of-the-moment phone call to the then owner, Mrs. Mary Hampson, as I was passing through town in the spring of 1985. With me was my wife, and her presence, as it turned out, was to prove crucial to what I may term the success of the visit.

Though by then deep in study for this book, I was not in

pursuit of anything specific in the old house. Perhaps I felt, somewhat vaguely and purely on instinct, that knowledge of its interior arrangements might help bring alive for me the personalities of the original occupants. But I did not expect to find at so late a date any documents or other untapped sources of information. Certainly I never anticipated how intimately, in another way, and even starkly, the old place would link itself to the very theme of the following chapters. That it did so, I trust, may serve as sufficient excuse for the personal tone of what follows.

We reached the house in midafternoon, turned into the grounds between the ancient wooden posts of the front gate, and walked up the flagstone path to the high front door. As we went, a thin voice called softly, and we turned to see sitting on a side porch a small, frail-looking woman. Gray hair flying loosely, an ashen, though expressive face, and pathetically gnarled, arthritic hands formed my immediate impression. This first sight of Mrs. Hampson set me to wondering again why she had permitted our visit. More than forty years before, she and her husband had inherited the property from Martha Dickinson, Emily's niece, but for three decades now she had lived there alone as a widow. Her age was usually put at about ninety, and it was reported that she had no great liking for literary intruders, in fact had very few visitors of any kind.

Entering the house through a narrow porch door flanking the front entrance, we found ourselves in a wide, high-ceilinged central hallway that ran straight back from the front door. Dark-paneled walls and, above the paneling, a plush wallpaper of dark red, peeling here and there, gave a peculiar effect of age and gloom, even decay. Further in, against the left-hand wall, was a staircase, broad but not grand. Its red-carpeted flight mounted straight up to a landing on the second floor, where it veered around to the right.

At the landing stood a closed door, apparently leading to more rooms at the back of the house.

As we walked along the hall, a glimpse through the wide doors on either side, leading to parlor and library, showed that both rooms were scattered around with much furniture of old-time design. Visible in them also, and something of a shock to encounter, was a blizzard of debris—papers of all sorts and sizes, lying loose or stuffed in envelopes, along with books, newspapers, and magazines—all spilled and thrown in disorderly heaps everywhere on floors, tables, and chairs. The lengthy surface of the heavy library table held a virtual avalanche of such papers.

Beyond the stairway we entered a small dining room. Here the walls were papered in royal blue, making the atmosphere nearly as somber as the hallway. A ponderous square table took up the room's center, and around the walls stood a random assortment of old chests and cabinets. Aiming a finger at the ceiling, Mrs. Hampson explained that the ornate, exposed beams were a wedding gift to Austin from his friends in town. Her offhand, familiar air in speaking of the fact made it seem something that had happened only yesterday. From a corner cupboard she took two, squat-stemmed wineglasses and set them on the table, saying we must drink some port. As she went searching for a bottle I bent down to have a closer look at the glasses, which were of an unusual cut. When I saw that each was encased in a film of ancient dust I made a sign to my wife and said thank you, but it was too early in the day for us. With a curious sigh of disappointment Mrs. Hampson invited us to take seats at the table.

She was in a talkative mood and soon plunged into a stream of reminiscences about her travels in the twenties, including several trips to Europe. Alternating between laughter and indignation, she told at some length of the

French customs officials who had insisted on taking photographs of her left ear. Then she veered around to subjects closer to home. Concentrating on her friend and benefactor Martha Dickinson, with evident sincerity she insisted that Martha was a better writer than her famous poet-aunt but that her many novels, stories, and poems had been cruelly ignored. "Emily wrote well, too," she conceded, "but she was sometimes too Mother Goosey." The unexpected phrase, cleverly identifying the subtle flaw in many of Emily's lesser verses, made my wife and me laugh outright. Emily, too, I felt sure, would have laughed to hear criticism so pointedly expressed, even of her own work.

Spread on the table before us were a few yellowed old magazines, copies of the *Century*, the *Forum*, and *Scribner's*. They contained, as Mrs. Hampson proceeded to show us, some of Martha Dickinson's earliest writing, dating to the turn of the century. "Did Martha talk much about Emily?" I asked as I went through the brittle pages. Especially in Emily's later years, I knew, her niece had been as close to her as anyone, paying her almost daily visits (a fact that has been rather deliberately obscured in Dickinson biography). At Emily's death in 1886 Martha had been a mature twenty, so she should have had many clear memories of those sad last days.

"Martha never talked to me about Emily."

Given the woman's long and close acquaintance with the niece, and Martha's intimacy with her famous aunt, that hardly seemed possible. Martha had, after all, written two books of reminiscences about Emily. In my surprise I pressed the point. "Never? Not at all?"

Annoyance tinged her voice. "I said she *never* talked to me about her aunt."

My surprise still held me. "You mean she refused?"

"I never asked," she flashed back, then deliberately swung back to face my wife, taking up again the thread of her youthful days in Europe. The warnings I had received about her unpredictable, often acerbic manner were true after all. Still, I decided, being ninety wasn't a bad excuse for occasional petulance.

As I listened to her voice drone on, I looked around at the ancient furnishings and was struck anew by the melancholy fact that this sturdy old house of so much early promise, linked for so long to one of America's finest poets, should have ended as the domain of a virtual stranger. Beneath this roof, in this very room, the youthful Emily had passed many contented hours, possibly the happiest of her life. Here her poems had found, in her sister-in-law's delighted response, their first and most discriminating praise. How wry a twist of fate to have it all come down to this poor, lone woman who, though enjoying a direct link to the poet, refused even to talk of her.

At least the house itself was still standing, and apparently in good condition structurally. An Italianate villa built by the elder Dickinson in 1856 to keep his talented son Austin from leaving Amherst, in its day it was considered quite sumptuous. During its first forty years of existence, up to Austin's death in 1895, few if any changes had been made in it. Eighteen years later, at the death of Austin's wife, Susan, it had passed still unaltered to Martha, who, until her own death in 1943, spent much of her time living and traveling abroad. As the property of the Hampsons the house has been left intact, so that today it stands almost exactly as it stood at the start, even to much of the furniture. This unusual state of preservation, both inside and out, was graphically recalled in the late thirties by a visitor who remembered it from a first visit she had paid fifty years before, while Austin was still alive. Writing to Martha afterward, she said she had found the familiar rooms "a door into the past . . . the one place where time had stood still."

I looked across the table at Mrs. Hampson, her faded eyes now alight in the stream of memories she was directing at my sympathetic wife. It was plain to see that the woman could not have a great many years left. When she was gone what would become of the Evergreens? Of course it was not a subject to be broached directly, so in a pause of the talk I ventured what I thought was an innocent question. "This big house must be lonely for you. Do you have any children who visit?"

Her head turned swiftly as she snapped her reply. "No! I would never have children because you lose your own life then. I wanted my independence, to do just as I wished. Having children would have been horrible!" A bit unsteadily she stood up, smoothed down the skirt of her dress, and asked if I would like to see the other rooms. It was clear that my question had nettled her, and without waiting for a reply she turned and started for the door.

In the disorderly library she carefully threaded her way through the jumble of furniture, stepping gingerly around the ragged piles of paper debris (a glance showed that the mixture included many old letters, legal documents, and even ancient household bills). Resting a bony hand on the back of a thin-ribbed rocking chair, she invited me to have a seat. I was to take my time, she said, and have a good look at anything that interested me. Then she took my wife by the arm and steered her into the hallway. "Now, Dorothy," she whispered as they went, "we'll go into the kitchen so we can talk and have those nice cakes you brought."

A low stack of books lay on the floor beside the chair. I sat down and picked one up, and found it was the first volume of a biography of the Dickinson's great friend Sam Bowles. The flyleaf was inscribed from Sue to Austin in the year of publication, 1885. Close behind me was a shelf crammed with books and papers. I reached over and pulled down a small, thick volume bound in black leather. It was Martha's own Bible, its pages holding a small photo of her mother and a holy card of the Blessed Virgin. On the same shelf lay several books of philosophy and theology, all with Sue's name written in. From the welter of papers on the long table I extracted a small brown leather notebook. It was a diary kept by Martha during a trip to France in 1903, its diminutive pages mostly recording daily meetings in Paris with Captain Alexander Bianchi. Here was true poignance, for Amherst rumor had long insisted, though lacking proof, that Martha's marriage to Bianchi had been a sorry one. The captain, it was said, after spending a great deal of Martha's money, had one day simply disappeared. It was only a few minutes later that, among the papers strewn along the table, I came across proof of the rumor. A court document showed that in 1920 Martha had been granted a divorce on grounds of desertion, stated as occurring in 1908.

Suddenly I was disturbingly aware of the heavy, almost sullen atmosphere of the library, and though ordinarily unbothered by such dusty surroundings, I now for some reason began to feel suffocated. To change my mood, I left the library and wandered back along the hallway to a second parlor or drawing room in which the clutter appeared less extreme. Going in, I stopped at a side table to finger listlessly through a small mound of old letters, opening several. What I read did not help my mood.

One letter, dated 1898 and still in its original envelope, brought to Susan condolences on the death from heart trouble of her eldest son, the epileptic Ned. Another, dated 1883, also still in its envelope, affected me even more strongly, for it offered sympathy on the death of Susan's younger son, eight-year-old Gilbert. It was the sudden passing of this beloved little boy, always called Gib, along with the effect of the tragedy on all concerned, that formed the basis of the theory I had for several years been pursuing.★

As I conceived it, the death of Gib had created a wave of repercussions immediately felt in both houses, effects that went well beyond what was presently understood in Dickinson biography. Emily herself it had helped to rob not only of health—so much had long been understood—but of her newly revived hope of becoming a published poet, and in addition had snuffed out all her happily renewed plans for a late marriage with Judge Otis Lord. Austin it had cruelly twisted. At a stroke, it had turned him into an embittered seeker of revenge against the fate that had taken his boy, a revenge he quickly found in the arms of Mabel Loomis Todd, a married neighbor half his age. Mrs. Todd, first editor of his sister's poetry, previously for him had been little more than a pleasant companion, though perhaps with the added spice of possible indiscretion in the background. Austin's fall, in its turn, had given rise to one of the most lamentable episodes in American literature, even yet not ended: the deliberate wrecking, by Mabel Todd, of Sue Dickinson's reputation as wife and mother in order to justify Austin's defection and to excuse her own role in the triangle.

All of this I had hoped to demonstrate, and at the time of my visit to Austin's house I was still considering whether to take the theory one fairly radical step further, bending to the inescapable pressure, as it seemed to me, of the evidence. Emily, it very much appeared, already a hopeless invalid, crushed by her own sense of loss as woman and artist, and

---

★ "several years"—actually about fifteen years, since shortly after completion of my biography *The Hidden Life of Emily Dickinson*, published in 1971. At the time of my earlier studies the relevant documents—those drawn on for the present book—were unavailable, still closely held by the daughter of Mabel Todd. They were not released until after publication of Richard Sewall's two-volume biography of Emily Dickinson in 1974.

by the newest tragedy next door, believing she had not long to live in any case, had ended by taking her own life.

Now, as I stood in the gloom of the Evergreens, reading that hundred-year-old letter with Gib's name inked on the page only days after his funeral, it all came suddenly, grippingly alive for me. But that was only the prelude. Within minutes of restoring the letter to its pile I was to encounter an even more graphic reminder of all that the death of little Gib had meant, in both this house and the one next door.

The high-pitched sound of female laughter, mingling the voices of both women, echoed along the hallway. Mrs. Hampson, I judged, was now in a more relaxed frame of mind, so I crossed to the dining room to find the two back at the table and chatting happily. But as I entered the room, a glance of irritation replaced the smile on the pathetically lined face, and I hesitated in the doorway—upon which Mrs. Hampson rose from her chair and came toward me, saying I must now have a look upstairs. "I'll be gone only a moment," she said over her shoulder to my wife, who barely managed to suppress a laugh at my being so handily shunted off again.

What Mrs. Hampson called Sister Sue's room stood exactly over the main parlor below. But it was obviously no longer in use, having no beds, only a huddle of chipped and forlorn old bureaus at the center, piled around with chairs, tables, and several old trunks. There she left me with a rather curt invitation to have a leisurely look all around this upper floor.

I turned to the mantelpiece where I saw perched a torn old shoebox, lifted the lid, and uncovered a jumble of old photographs, some in frames, some bare. On top was one that showed a serious-faced Ned Dickinson, dapper in riding pants, boots, bowler, and mustache. In the biographies of his aunt this young man was scarcely more than a shadow, but here he was as he had looked to her in life, a vital, loved presence. Near the bottom of the box was a slightly larger photograph from which looked up the sweetly smiling face of golden-haired Gib.

The two other bedrooms on that upper floor I found to be appropriately furnished, and more or less in order. Coming to the rear wall, at the head of the wide staircase, I recognized the closed door as the same one I had earlier glimpsed from below. It was locked, but the key was in the latch, and I hesitated only a moment. As the door swung open I saw stretching away from me a long, narrow corridor, dark now in the waning afternoon. I stepped in.

First on the left was a room with a small, oblong window opening on the corridor, not a common feature for the inside of a house. Through the dusty glass I caught sight of simple furniture set neatly around the walls. The door proved to be tightly shut, however, and I didn't want to try forcing it. Next on the left was an ordinary storeroom. Then came the usual back stairway leading down to the kitchen. Opposite was the door to the attic proper, in which I could see were stored some old bedsteads and odd bits of furniture. A large wicker basket under a table set me to thinking where I could have seen it before, and in a moment I recalled: in the foreground of a well-known photograph of the Dickinsons and friends on returning from a picnic. (Days later I was able to verify my memory—the outing was to Shutesbury, the year 1882.)

Turning back along the corridor I came again to the room with the oblong window, and this time I couldn't resist giving the door a harder shove, putting my shoulder to it. When it gave a little, I pushed again, and on squeaky hinges it swung fully open. The light in the room came dimly filtering in at the far wall, through the four panes of a single, dust-smudged window. But I could see that, alone at the room's center, there stood two children's playthings, a tricycle and a full-sized rocking horse. From the way they stood isolated in their own space, facing each other head-on, it seemed as if they had been in use only minutes before by two little boys in full charge.

The tricycle looked to be in good condition except that the bare iron seat was slightly askew. For wheels it had not rubber tires but the broad, flat iron rims common a century ago. The rocking horse had a coat of light gray felt, also in good condition, with a bushy yellow mane hanging stiffly along the high, curved neck. I put a hand on the rump and gently pressed, and the little horse began to rock, smoothly, but with a slight creaking each time the proud head came up.

After Gib's death in 1883 no other little boys had lived in this house, of that I was certain. Judging by the other things in the room, the small cupboards, the chests, and the closets—the oblong window especially, which allowed inspection from the outside—this room might once have been a nursery. Later perhaps it had served as the growing Gib's own room (the three regular upstairs bedrooms would have been used by his parents and by Ned and Martha). In one corner stood the only item not usual in a nursery, a brass bed, a single apparently for a grown-up. Had the weary Susan rested on it, or Austin, while keeping vigil through Gib's feverish last hours?

It didn't seem reasonable or even likely that the room could have been left so long unused or unaltered, so that it stood now as it was on the day Gib's wasted body was carried out. Yet as I looked around in the gathering dusk, that was the definite impression that gripped me, and from what I knew of the stricken people involved it didn't seem so wild an idea. During the intervening hundred years the house had been in the hands of only five different owners, all family, or closely connected, none of whom would have felt any urgency to interfere with such an out-of-the-way chamber. Three of the five might well have preferred to keep it as it was on that last mournful day.

Or was I being too easily convinced, conjuring up ghosts of my own? Quite probably, I decided, and a very human tendency after all, given the spell cast by the old house, as well as the strangely compelling nature of the whole Dickinson saga. I was seeing what I wanted to see, no doubt of it.

But that careful conclusion had hardly taken form in my mind when I found my attitude swinging back the other way again. Was I being overly objective? Was I seeking the safety of a soberer, more practical view because I felt embarrassed by sentimental notions barely acceptable in a novel? There was nothing so very improbable, I told myself, about a bereaved family permanently shutting a door on its most tragic memory, preserving the site as a pathetic memorial to the enormity of a loss never expected. Such things have been known to happen.

For a few moments I stood there, feeling acutely uncertain as well as uncomfortable, finding nothing that would enable me to tip the balance either way. I threw a final, indecisive glance around the room, letting my gaze linger on rocking horse and tricycle. Then I walked softly out, pulled the door shut behind me, retraced my steps along the narrow corridor, then shut and locked the outer door.

Going down the stairs to the first floor, I decided I would say nothing to Mrs. Hampson about the little room.

When that which is, and that which was,
Apart, intrinsic stand—
And this brief tragedy of flesh
Is shifted like a sand.

EMILY DICKINSON

I

Home Is a Holy Thing

A WEEK OR SO before the arrival of her fifty-second birth-day, Emily Dickinson unexpectedly found herself facing one of those small, familiar moments in life that, soon or late, seem to visit almost everyone. A photograph showing her niece, the fifteen-year-old Martha, in a fetching head-and-shoulders pose had been sent over for her inspection from her brother's house next door. Something in the picture—the quiet self-confidence of the hinted, sidelong smile, or the way the girl's hat with its circular brim gave the effect of a halo worn jauntily—stirred Emily to a rare personal admission. "That's the little girl I always meant to be, but wasn't," she wrote Martha's mother on returning the photo, "the very hat I always meant to wear, but didn't, and the attitude toward the universe so precisely my own, that I feel very much as if I were returning Elisha's Horses, or the Vision of John at Patmos." Even in its guise as affectionate banter the remark is arresting. Underneath more rueful than merry, it is Emily's outspoken recognition of the fact that her own attitude toward the universe, once so exuberant, had drastically altered.

When Emily wrote those words to her sister-in-law, in

December 1882, she had already passed into the recluse of legend, her life firmly set in what she must have guessed was to be its final pattern. Her last hope for a change to a more normal existence, the contemplated late marriage with old family friend Judge Otis Lord, had been cruelly dashed with the severe stroke suffered by the seventy-year-old Lord that May. By now both her parents were dead, her father for a decade, her mother having died just the month before, and only her younger sister, Vinnie, with whom she had always been close, remained to share the house with her. Poetry had become no more than an occasional concern, mostly revision of her old work or the gathering of finished manuscripts into a series of sewn packets. No longer did she think seriously of trying to publish any of the heaped verses— some seventeen hundred short poems, the product of nearly thirty years' writing—that lay in her bureau drawer. Except when she visited her brother's family next door, or took a nighttime stroll through the tree-studded Dickinson property, her physical world was wholly contained within the ample walls of the big, redbrick house on Main Street.

This reclusive existence, however—it can stand emphasizing—was not at all a matter of brooding isolation. By means of her steady involvement with the busy, active life of her brother's family next door she had a regular part, if at a considerable remove, in all the bustle and concern of everyday village and household affairs. Her brother Austin, a leader in the life of town and college, and a lawyer of wide experience, dropped in frequently at the Mansion with his stock of news. Her sister-in-law, the former Susan Gilbert, a woman of intellect as well as a homemaker of taste, was a reader whose range of interests matched and in one area, science, exceeded Emily's own (it is somehow a bit startling to find that Susan, a year before her death in 1913 at age eighty-three, expressed strong interest in the then brand-new general relativity theory of Einstein). While Susan's attention was often taken up by the needs of her growing family, the intimacy between her and Emily, begun when both were teenagers, after forty years was still (all assertions to the contrary notwithstanding) close and confiding.

But it was with the three children of the Evergreens, even more than with their parents, that Emily now found her chief delight. First of the three was Edward, or Ned, named for Emily's father. Then twenty years old and a student at Amherst College, Ned was sensitive, bookish, of a pronounced idealistic, even chivalric temperament, and keenly aware of his position in the long line of distinguished Amherst Dickinsons. With his aunt Emily he frequently shared confidences, particularly his discoveries in books, as well as his fascination with politics and world affairs. These last are topics not often named as occupying Emily, yet it is reported that whenever her nephew brought word of some important happening she listened "with greedy interest." In these latter years of her life it was mainly, as his sister said afterward, through Ned that Emily "found her window on the outside world," which often included, again in Martha's phrase, "the ludicrous and droll side of things." An epileptic, Ned faced the seriousness of his disability only as he reached his mid-teens, and even then it did not hamper his taking part in such strenuous activities as horseback riding and tennis. His pleasure in these sports, too, he shared with his aunt, who had her own fond memories of horseback rides through the countryside.

Martha Dickinson, known as Mattie, early showing something of her mother's bright charm and lithe intelligence, had already begun to develop the literary leanings that were to make her, early in the new century, a published novelist in her own right. Between her and Emily there had quickly grown up a special bond as they "talked of serious or imaginative things, situations in books, or wondered about the future, gravely comparing our absurdly unequal conclusions, without a sign on her part of the crudity of mine." In those social matters vital to a growing girl, Emily was also quick to show sympathy. "Did you love the party, dear?" Martha remembered her aunt's inquiring more than once, and when the reply was tepid, finishing with "I see— coroner's verdict—dead!" Allowed the freedom of Emily's room in the Mansion from the age of two or three, Martha was not prevented by this long familiarity from sensing that her aunt was somehow different. As she expressed it afterward, her aunt Emily had always been set apart by reason of an "indefinite quality" that clung around her like an aura.

It was also Martha who left on record perhaps the most evocative, certainly the most reliable, firsthand description of Emily as she was in her last years before failing health slowed and changed her: "She was of medium height, decisive in manner, not frail or suggestive of ill health. . . . She often moved about in a sort of revery of her own—flitting always—and quick as a trout if disturbed. Her low-pitched voice was the instrument of an unconscious artist, almost husky at times of intensity." Two points in that deft portrait, both easily overlooked, deserve emphasis. Emily's personality was not tentative, not uncertain or vacillating, and she was decidedly not fey. Further, despite the leaning toward reverie, she was physically energetic, not ethereal, unearthly, or frail. The low, husky voice was noted by others—some recalled it as "breathless"—but only Martha took note of how it was employed as an "instrument," consciously or otherwise, suggesting an interesting link to the deft speech patterns and voice sounds of her poetic technique.

The last of the children in the house next door was the fair-haired, blue-eyed Thomas Gilbert, called Gib after his own hurried pronunciation of the name. The child of his parents' maturer years, Gib was born when Sue was forty-four, an event especially gratifying to Austin, who dearly wished a healthy male heir to companion the epileptic Ned. In a remarkable degree, Gib possessed a precocious charm of mind and manner that captivated all who spent even a few minutes in his whirlwind presence. Besides a winning frankness and simplicity, there was in him, as a neighbor recalled, "a self-reliance rare in a boy so gentle and sensitive, which seemed, somehow, to lift him into the sphere of men. He became not only interesting but companionable." That such a boy should have a strong attraction for Emily—herself so often appealingly childlike—is not surprising, nor that she should be captivated by what early proved to be Gib's ready tongue. With positive glee her letters repeatedly take note of her nephew's childishly clever remarks. "Talk of 'hoary Reprobates!'" she summed up for Sue at one point, "your urchin is more antique in wiles than the Egyptian Sphinx."

Gentle as he was, Gib had already begun to exhibit a willful streak—the Dickinson independence, it was indulgently called—but even in this flaw his aunt could find only reason for admiration. If Gib's parents went for a carriage ride without him, Emily wrote almost proudly, "his piercing cries of 'Go cadgie' . . . rend the neighborhood." If the boy indulged in some tiny rage of refusal against a parental order, emphasized by what Emily called his "pretty execrations," even then in the eyes of his doting aunt he was "lovely as a stubborn bird." Long afterward, when little Gib had been dead half a century, his sister fondly recalled him as both "willful and winsome."

With one or another of these three running in to see her almost daily, seeking sympathy or encouragement or a cohort, with her congenial brother and her best friend only a

step away, and with the constant companionship of her
books, Emily's days could in no sense be considered bleak
or empty. On that wintry day approaching Christmas 1882
she had reached a large measure of accommodation to her
confined life, even, it might be said, a degree of grateful
acceptance. No longer was she the yearning artist who had
so confidently planned to make her family "proud—
sometime," as she said, by becoming "distinguished." No
longer was she the forlorn young woman caught by her
hopeless love for a married man—so much may be said even
while the man's identity continues in doubt. As frequently
happens with those who have attained a certain age, artists
no less than ordinary folks, Emily had at length awakened
to her good fortune in possessing, in devoted family and
comfortable home, a satisfying niche in the world. Happiness for her, now, grew not from the cultivation of personal
excellence but largely from the simple enjoyment of the
ordinary human things of every day. Feeling real con-
tentment—even if laced with resignation—she was able to
look steadily at a future that, while it lacked the old excitement, was both secure and in its own way promising.

At age fifty-two Emily was no longer the slim, eager-
eyed young woman to be seen in the old daguerreotype, but
she was still in good health and could reasonably expect to
live at least another decade—her father had survived to
seventy-one, robust to the last, her mother, though finally
disabled by a stroke, to seventy-eight. She might well anticipate the pleasure of being on hand to see both Ned and
Martha take hold in the world, could hope to see little Gib
reach manhood. Here was some compensation for all she
had lost, or given up, or never achieved.

But it was not to be. Sadly, fate had something much
more somber in prospect for the ending of Emily's story.
Remaining to her in that winter of 1882 were little more

than three years, no one of which was to be without emotional strain, at times severe. During her final eighteen months she would find herself condemned to carry the heavy burden of invalidism, for long stretches being confined to bed or chair. Finally, and in a way worst of all, she would become a helpless witness to the rapid disintegration of the happy family across the way, piteously marring one of her earliest and dearest dreams.

Thirty years before, in a letter to her brother, Emily had dwelt fondly on the idea of home. To her it was "a holy thing," and she added her earnest belief that "nothing of doubt or distrust can enter its blessed portals . . . here seems indeed to be a bit of Eden which not the sin of any can utterly destroy." It was a sentiment fully shared by her brother, who at that same time was writing in similar strain to his fiancée, Susan Gilbert: "A home Sue! It's too beautiful a word for the world . . . the beautiful answering of the dearest dream." Through the years both brother and sister had held firmly to that ideal, sure that in their own ordered lives, and in their two houses so cozily neighboring, the dream had been completely and wonderfully realized.

Both were wrong. It was scarcely a month after Emily returned the photograph of her niece to Susan that the dream began to crumble as there came sniffing at the portals of the Evergreens the very evils Emily had named: first doubt, then outright distrust, and at last actual sin.

★   ★   ★

WITH THE ARRIVAL of the new year of 1883 word reached Emily, probably by way of Martha, that all was not well in the house next door. The nature of the trouble must have surprised her, for it does not seem to have had much if any precedent. Late in January, Susan Dickinson, in some manner not known, accused her husband of paying too much attention, of a very personal sort, to a pretty, vivacious neighbor, a married woman half his age. Complicating matters, the young woman in question—who stood accused of encouraging the attention—was no stranger to the Dickinson parlor. Just over a year before, as the wife of a young professor newly arrived at the college, Mabel Loomis Todd had been warmly welcomed into the society of the Evergreens, her sprightly manner and artistic talents rapidly earning her a position as a favorite of the whole family.

Though Emily had not met the new neighbor, she would have heard a good deal about her from the people at the Evergreens, with emphasis on the woman's impressive talents (singer, pianist, painter, budding writer). The gallant Ned, especially, had been smitten by her charm and intelligence, and he was soon seizing every opportunity to be in her company. His sister Mattie, wholeheartedly accepting Mrs. Todd as the perfect model of accomplished womanhood, was also quickly under her spell. While Mrs. Todd had in that first year been many times a guest at the Evergreens, on only a single occasion had she entered Emily's house. In September 1882, at Vinnie's invitation, Austin had walked her over after a lunch at the Evergreens. Greeted enthusiastically by Vinnie, she spent an hour playing and singing in the back parlor, Emily all the while remaining out of sight. When the musical session ended, Emily had sent the maid in with a glass of wine and a brief, handwritten poem. Though she had declined a meeting, she could not withhold all sign of recognition from this engaging new friend of her brother's family.

The wording of the charge Susan leveled at Austin—and Mabel—that January has not survived. Yet enough is known so that the incident itself, along with the steps leading to it, may be reconstructed in some detail. Fittingly, the principal documents that make this possible are the diaries and journals kept by Mrs. Todd herself—Mabel, as she was soon being called by the older Dickinsons.

Arriving in Amherst with her husband late in the summer of 1881, Mabel had soon become friendly with many of the college faculty, but especially with the Dickinsons. Encouraged by her receptive hosts, she began paying frequent, then almost daily visits to their house. Often she was accompanied by her husband, attending more or less formal gatherings, but increasingly she went there on her own to play and sing for the family, to give music lessons to Mattie, or just to enjoy the comfort of the big house and grounds, so much more pleasant than her own cramped rooms in a nearby boardinghouse. After each visit she was escorted home by one of the Dickinson men, usually Ned, occasionally Austin himself. So completely did she captivate the whole family of Dickinsons that long before the close of her first year in Amherst, she was being included in nearly all their country outings and regular carriage rides. With Sue she became as great a favorite as she was with the others, valued in particular for her ability to stimulate talk and gaiety in a group, as well as provide musical entertainment. A characteristically bubbly letter Sue wrote her some three months before the January troubles, while she was at her parents' home in Washington, D.C., shows better than anything else how much a part of life at the Evergreens the scintillating Mabel had become:

Dear Toddy,

The world seems wrong without you and most [word illegible]. We talked about it over our Sunday dinner from which we have just come and decided Mr Todd ought not to have taken you away. . . . Perhaps with such advice you will turn back. Life here has simmered down to winter elements . . . we have had a three-day's pour which has hurled everybody in upon interior resources most forcibly—even ones nearest neighbors become as remote as well could be. . . .

Sept. 28th. Dear Toddy I left you to go for a drive with Austin and I have just got back—that is I have been to Boston and a party at the Crowells and have sat up a night with dear Ned who had a tussle for breath the result of a midnight drive to Northampton in the rain. . . . I found your insubstantial thought of me on my bureau Tues. eve when I returned from Boston. I am charmed that your memory and affection work so beautifully together. . . . The party at the Crowells was nice but rather lifeless. No "thoughts of flame." Mrs. Martin was elegant in a new costume but so monotonous! Oh bring back—bring back—bring back my Toddins to me!

The first outward sign that Austin had conceived a more than neighborly interest in the newcomer appeared in November 1882 while Sue was out of town on an extended trip, having gone to visit a married brother in Michigan. The incident occurred on the seventh of that month and involved Austin's taking Mabel alone for an unusually long carriage ride, some four hours, their route leading the pair all through the Pelham hills, then in their autumn dress. When Sue returned from Michigan ten days later she learned rather promptly of her husband's outing, and immediately sensed something besides gallantry in the wind. A few days afterward, when Mabel came to the Evergreens for an evening of whist, it was not Ned but his father who saw her home through the cold, blustery night. On his return, another guest teased him about his willingness to leave his warm fireside for the young woman, and this brought from Sue a veiled comment of the sort that, transparently, intends the opposite of what it says. "For pity's sake don't laugh at him. If there is one person he actually likes I am too rejoiced."

Undaunted, Austin soon followed up on the opening

given him by the carriage ride. For the Christmas 1882 holidays Mabel and her husband went to her parents' home in Washington, but before they left, Austin managed to be alone with Mabel on several other occasions. Twice the two had leisurely walks together along the outskirts of town, and on the day of her departure for Washington he again took her for a solitary ride, this time in the family sleigh. On its conclusion he deposited her at the railway station, where she joined her patiently waiting husband. No special effort was made by Austin to hide any of these meetings, apparently, so that Sue's reaction initially would have been no more than severe annoyance over a husband making a fool of himself in public. But then, with Mabel gone, more direct and specific charges surfaced, all the more disturbing because of their source. It was Sue's son Ned who first made an issue of his father's conduct with Mrs. Todd.

In the week before Christmas 1882, or possibly just after, Ned confessed to his mother something of his own intense feeling for Mabel. Exactly how he phrased his admission, or under what circumstances he made it, are not known, but he certainly would have included the fact that the woman had, once at least, admitted that she "cared" for him, and several times at his request had worn his college fraternity pin. These things would probably have been enough to stir in Sue a measure of indignation, but then Ned went further. Now, he said, Mrs. Todd had grown tired of toying with him and had bent her sights on someone else, none other than his own reserved and upright father. No doubt he gave additional details of the carriage rides and the long walks together, along with any other facts he had observed or which Mabel had let slip in conversation. Sue, perhaps slightly disbelieving, began casting back over the events of the previous year, noting casual things that had drawn no special notice at the time, especially how often her husband

and Mabel had managed to go off together when in groups on outings.

The very day of Mabel's arrival back in Amherst, January 6, 1883, Austin contrived to meet her twice. Supposedly by accident, he encountered her carriage on its way home from the station and waved it to a stop to greet both husband and wife. That same evening, before the Todds had fairly settled in, he paid a call on them in their boardinghouse parlor. Next day, a Sunday, brought the Todds down to the Evergreens for tea, certainly at the invitation of both Sue and Austin, and immediately Mrs. Todd was aware of a change in her hostess's attitude. The coolness was so marked that Mabel felt she had to ask about it directly, but just what she said, or how or when, is lost. In any case, her diary shows that the following morning—with Austin gone up to Boston on business—Sue paid her a visit, the first time Mrs. Dickinson had made the trip up the hill to the boardinghouse. Alone, the two women had a frank talk, later styled by Mabel as "a long conversation which was conducted with fairness (in general) on both sides."

Whatever explanations Mabel offered that morning, they proved sufficient—probably it was not difficult to show that Ned's worried tale was no more than the overheated imaginings of innocently enamored youth. The contrite Sue, as if trying to make up for her moment of distrust, during the next three weeks did what she could to repair the friendship. With elegant afternoon teas, gay sleighing parties that ended at the Dickinson house for hot chocolate, musical evenings, concerts at the college, carriage rides, and simple quiet gatherings for talk and card playing, through most of January hardly a day passed when Mabel was not in the Dickinsons' company. Then, abruptly, in the first days of February, everything unraveled once more.

All that can be known explicitly of the second break

between the families, both date and cause, is contained in a remark to be found in Mabel's journal. "Another slight misunderstanding has occurred," she wrote on February 3, "which has temporarily overclouded us. But I'm sure it will pass away. Only the old, cordial, frank relations I am afraid can never be resumed." (Possibly pertinent is the fact that on successive evenings, February 1 and 2, Austin was at the boardinghouse, both times with Mabel alone.) Mabel's estimate of the new troubles, however, considerably understated matters. By now, for some reason, Sue was convinced that her son had spoken the truth and that Mabel posed a very real threat to the peace and good order of her home. Austin, doing little to calm his wife's fears, on that same evening of February 3, again trudged through the snow to pass an evening with the Todds. He was, as Mabel noted, "exceedingly bright and entertaining."

Mabel was right in guessing that her accustomed easy relations with Sue had been permanently damaged. Increasingly from that time she became a source of bitterness and dissension in the Dickinson household, a situation which did not spare Ned or Mattie. Of Austin's attitude it can only be said that dismissing his son's charges as boyish exaggeration, he simply denied there was anything wrong in his relations with the Todds, and would continue to see them, or either of them, when and as he wished.

There was some justification, it must be said, in Austin's making a claim of total freedom in his choice of friends. As was well known to Sue and to most others in town, he already enjoyed quite free and apparently blameless public friendships with several of the college faculty wives, even taking them alone for drives in the country. Admittedly, it was an unusual arrangement, but he was supported in it by the forceful example of the Dickinson's great friend Sam Bowles, influential editor of the *Springfield Republican*. A frequent and always welcome visitor to the Evergreens until his death in 1878, Bowles, too, had been known for his many untrammeled friendships among the women of his acquaintance, married and unmarried, and everyone, including Bowles's wife, appeared to accept and approve the situation as normal. So prominent were these female friendships in Bowles's life that his biographer felt it wise to allude to the fact: "He was a man who could unite an entire and life-long loyalty to one woman, the partner of his life, the mother of his children, and the mistress of his home, with intimate and mutually helpful friendships with other women." A whole page of discussion emphasizing the intellectual and spiritual qualities of Bowles's women friends follows, concluding with: "In the homage he paid there was nothing of perilous sentiment, no philandering or flirtation." Here arose Sue's dilemma, such as it was, for she could not easily reject for her own husband the freedom she was known to have approved in their admired friend.

Yet she was worried enough that she wished at least to put a stop to Mabel's access to the Evergreens, and in this she succeeded. For the ensuing three months, until Mabel again left Amherst for Washington in April, Austin saw her only in the parlor of the boardinghouse, occasionally in public for walks and rides. Twice in those three months they met in the parlor of the Mansion, where Mabel sang and played at Vinnie's request, both times Emily again declining to join the little group. That Emily was thoroughly aware of all the bad feeling hardly needs proof. The strain and tension must have repeatedly generated worried talk among all members of both families, and Mattie, if not Ned, would surely have kept her informed.

For seven weeks during late April and May 1883 Mabel was again out of Amherst, enjoying her usual "brilliant" holiday, as she called it, in Washington. Probably on the advice of her parents, while there she made another attempt at reconciliation with Sue, sending her a box of flowers. But it was a waste of effort, for Sue's response, rather predictably, was to ignore both gift and gesture. Instead of returning thanks, she deliberately made matters worse by sending a check, meant as payment for the piano lessons Mabel had voluntarily given Mattie.

By now opinions in both houses were divided. Ned, more than ever ready to believe Mabel culpable, sided with his mother, but Mattie, unable to picture her radiant friend as a coquette, took her father's part. Vinnie, as was inevitable, insisted stoutly that her brother was incapable of anything foolish or dishonorable. Then she went further and wrote Mabel in Washington a note of encouragement. Whether correctly or not, she assumed that Mrs. Todd's departure from town had resulted from pressures exerted by the resentful Susan. "It's too bad prudence exiles you from so many friends," she wrote. "I think if the real reason of your absence was known there would be great indignation. I hope the days bring peace to you and that is healing." Vinnie's most likely source for that notion, of course, would have been Mabel herself.

In mid-May Mabel returned to Amherst—bringing with her for an extended visit both her mother and her grandmother—and found Sue's attitude as rigid as ever. It was at this juncture that Emily herself was drawn directly into the affair.

While not abundant, the evidence for Emily's role in the rapidly developing situation next door is more than circumstantial. It is comprised of two short notes, the true import of which Emily took pains to disguise but which are easily recognized as her personal effort to soothe ruffled feelings on both sides. Moved by the same sort of loyalty felt by her sister, though reluctantly and with a bit more subtlety, Emily too rallied to her brother's cause.

One note was intended for Susan, the other for Mabel, and probably they were dispatched at the same time. Both make reference to Shakespeare—cryptically in Susan's note, more openly in Mabel's—by invoking the classic jealousy tale of *Othello*. Sent with flowers, Emily's advice to Mabel tries to persuade her that Susan should not be judged harshly just because she had acted the part of a loving if overly suspicious wife: "Why should we censure Othello, when the Criterion Lover says 'Thou shalt have no other Gods before me'?" Sue's jealousy, she meant, no matter what its intensity or lack of real cause—as with Othello— was understandable after all, and so deserved to be forgiven. Mabel, reading those few veiled words just at that time, would have needed no special insight to grasp their plain meaning for her.

Emily's other note, to Susan, hides its real intent—in this case a mild disapproval—in a way that she also expected would be readily grasped by the recipient. It may, in fact, refer to some recent talk between the two women on the very subject of the Othello story: on April 11 in Boston, Austin attended a performance of the play with the great Salvini in the lead. He noted the fact in his diary and certainly would have talked of the experience on reaching home. In any case, that Emily's note was prompted by a specific occasion or incident, and is not the mere general censure it is now taken to be, becomes clear on even a casual reading: "Dear Sue—with the exception of Shakespeare, you have told me of more knowledge than anyone living— to say that sincerely is strange praise." Patently, Emily here relies for sense on some bit of shared knowledge, information left unstated but which she knows is common to herself and Susan. The words as they stand simply do not say enough, requiring the Othello reference for completion— the "exception" in Shakespeare. That further serious, even spirited talk between the two women resulted from the note, with Austin's behavior the sole topic, is likely. In that event, what may have been said poses no mystery. Emily wanted Sue to relent, to be once more her graceful self, and to welcome Mabel back into the society of her home.

Meantime, Vinnie took a more direct hand. To compensate for the ill feeling still emanating from the house next door—possibly with Emily's agreement, though this is very uncertain—she several times had the Todds, along with Mabel's mother and grandmother, over to the Mansion for an evening, also inviting Austin. On these occasions Emily, cautious about Sue's feelings as she waited for some sign of a change, chose to remain out of the way upstairs, incidentally again frustrating Mabel's rising hopes of meeting her.

The thaw finally occurred that summer, and it may have been a direct result of the pleading and urging of the two Dickinson sisters, with Mattie's voice added. Toward the end of June Mabel took her mother and grandmother to a vacation resort in New Hampshire where all three were to spend the summer months. While she was gone, Sue agreed that when Mabel returned to town in September, the Todds would again be welcomed into the pleasant bustle of life at the Evergreens. In effect she was admitting that the distasteful interlude of the past months had been not only unfortunate but unnecessary. She was conceding that after all, her jealousy had no real foundation, that in her suspicions she had simply been wrong.

Sue's change of heart quickly reached New Hampshire, by way of a letter from Mabel's husband. Gratefully, if guardedly, she entered the fact in her journal: "David . . .

writes that Mrs. Dickinson is lovely again, extended her hand pleasantly to him again, & talked cordially. And Mr. D. says everything is going all right for me. He *will have* it right. I suppose it will be long before things are on a really truthful, friendly basis. But I am sure, if there are no more accidents, that they will get back at last."

But Susan had not been wrong. Her instincts as wife and mother had served her well, and the mistake, a grievous one as all too soon it would prove, had been made by Emily and Vinnie. Had the two loyal sisters been able to see behind the scenes—specifically to look into the pages of Mabel's private journal, kept intermittently all during this period—they would assuredly have paused long before coming to the defense of either their brother or their clever young neighbor.

2

Mrs. Todd: Two Men for Me

THE PLAIN EVIDENCE of her own extensive and meticulous records shows that Mabel Todd was never quite, or was never only, the enthusiastic young innocent whose charm and talent impressed so many in Amherst. Her true outlook on people and affairs was much more calculated, and it had in addition a strangely skewed or unbalanced quality. In her journals, diaries, and letters she is shown to have been—stating the fact in its mildest, nontechnical form—a thoroughly self-absorbed, or better, self-contemplating, personality. Her simplest actions and opinions, and her ability, apparently unfailing, to captivate all whom she met, women as well as men, singly and in groups, were topics of which she never tired. Narcissism is the term that inevitably leaps to the mind of anyone who becomes at all familiar with the personality of Mabel Todd.

Excerpts from Mabel's journals have appeared before this, but the selections made, their brevity, and indeed their context and framing have tended to obscure, and on occasion distort, their true import. There are some documents—those tied to a rigid chronology, and of a certain length—that can be rightly judged only when scanned in full, or nearly so, and in proper sequence and setting, and this is emphatically the case with Mabel's journals.* In particular, her revealing memory of her first year's involvement with the Dickinson circle no descriptive summary or partial quotation can adequately reflect. What follows is the bulk of her various journal entries between January 1882 (six months after she first reached Amherst) and September 1883 (eight months after the first clash with Susan), a total of fifteen passages. Enough commentary is supplied to set each entry retrospectively in the flow of the narrative unfolded in the previous chapter, and to clarify offhand references.

As will become evident, the story told by these particular passages, when studied in sequence and in detail, is very different from anything that has so far appeared in print. So much may be stated at the outset.

It was at the home of her parents in Washington, D.C., that Mabel made her first relevant journal entry, on January 20, 1882. While it does not concern the Dickinsons directly, it is essential to an understanding of all that would develop in Amherst. On this day as Mabel lifts her pen she is twenty-five years old and has been married for three years. She has one child, a daughter named Millicent, whose care up to now has been shared with her mother and grandmother in Washington. That morning her husband David has just left for Amherst to resume his teaching duties at the college, a fact Mabel notes in opening the entry. She goes on:

> Everybody has been, as it were, "running after me"; and I have felt not the dawning, but the growth, intensely, of a wonderful social power. I cannot explain it, but I feel strength

* Her diaries, as distinct from her journals, were kept on a daily basis, for the most part merely listing the comings and goings of herself and others. The journals, written up every few weeks or months irregularly, gave her thoughts and activities more at length and more intimately.

and attractive power, & magnetism enough to fascinate a room full of people—which I have done, actually.

On New Year's day I was almost intoxicated with this power—which so overflowed and filled me, that our hundred callers seemed too small a company for it to be exercised upon. . . . I have flirted outrageously with every man I have seen—but in a way which David likes to have me, too. I have simply felt as if I could attract any man to any amount. If the power is wholly bottled up I get restless and feverish like a caged eagle, but if I exercise it in the innocent ways I *do*, I am satisfied—only that I sigh for more worlds to conquer. . . .

I have found such a dear friend. It is very romantic, and I cannot tell exactly how I came to find it yet; but Mr. Elliot, who was introduced to me by Madame Buel before my marriage, has always been very kind and complimentary to me. He has always paid me very pleasant attentions, and has, I know, admired me much. Lately he has seemed to avoid me a little, but the few times I have been with him, he has said very beautiful things to me, and I have found out that he is trying to outlive a strong love for me! . . . He is very lonely and says no man could reach his age—thirty-two—without having wished very much for love and tenderness. . . . When I thanked him for something he did for my comfort he said, "I would do *anything* for you," in a tone wherein a suppressed intensity of feeling [was] so strong that it was pitiful. . . . Heaven forbid that I should desire to exercise my power upon him. Although love and adulation and admiration are agreeable to me, and it will be a great trial to act simply, when I know I could keep him by using my attractiveness.

There followed an interruption of five weeks before her next entry, a long one, which was made after her return to Amherst. Dated March 2, 1882, it concerns almost entirely the first of her Amherst conquests, the susceptible Ned Dickinson, then a sophomore at the college. By now Mabel has become a regular at the Evergreens, and she and Ned

have been well acquainted for five months. To what extent
her extreme portrayal of Ned as a badly moonstruck admirer is accurate for the moment may be left open. That he
was strongly attracted to her at this time is true, but whether
she knew so early that he was an epileptic cannot be said:

> I have been at Mrs. Dickinson's a great deal since my
> return, & she admires me extravagantly, & praises me to Ned
> and Mattie all the time, as a sort of model for them. She
> appreciates me completely, and I love and admire her equally.
> She is a rare woman, & her home is my haven of pleasure in
> Amherst. Also, Ned and Mattie have run in to see me every
> day since my return. Then, too, I had not danced at all since
> my marriage, until this winter here, & I found that my waltz
> step did not go very well with the present fashion of waltzing
> so Ned undertook to teach me to get it better. Whenever I
> went to see Mrs. Dickinson there was a waltz in the hall with
> Ned, while Mattie played. . . . I never dreamed that Ned was
> more than ordinarily fond of me, or that I could be doing him
> any harm by allowing him to be my Knight Errant whenever
> David could not attend me. . . .
>
> I have known now, for a few days, that he [Ned] worships
> the very ground I walk on. He does not care now for general
> society, and only wants to sit near me and watch me. He is
> only a boy—only twenty—but he is the most graceful host
> in his own house that I have ever seen. And he is so very
> manly. . . .
>
> He told me the other day that until now his mother had
> more than filled every want in his life, but that he had come
> to think so much of me that it is his only thought . . . he
> knows he is restless and inattentive to his studies & thinking
> of me every moment. . . . One day he burst out with—"Oh!
> Mrs. Todd, I'm afraid I love you, & what shall I do?" I
> consoled him as well as I could by saying that he would get
> over it very soon. . . . He says he would do anything for

me—that I could twist him around my little finger—that he would go off and kill somebody if I bade him.

I told him that I was very fond of him and would always use what he called my "unlimited influence" over him for his good. "Ah!" he said, "What you are kind enough to call your affection for me is nothing for you to give; but I love you as you love your husband!" . . .

What can I do? He had plunged in irrevocably before I suspected it, and every time he sees me gay or brilliant in society, or sweet and tender to his mother, or tired after dancing, or kind to him, or in fact whenever and however he sees me, it adds to his love for me, & I cannot help it. He is perfectly innocent & pure about it, and has not an idea that he ought to root it out . . . he cannot see that it is wrong, & I certainly shall not open the knowledge of good and evil to him. . . .

Poor boy, poor boy! It is all an amazement to him. He is absolutely perfect in his habits, & is really a very strong and manly fellow, & remarkable in many ways. But that Heaven should bless me with the virgin love of a young man who hardly knows what has come to him, is very remarkable. . . . His mother does not know of it all, of course, and she thinks it is such a fine thing for her young son to have a "brilliant and accomplished married lady for his friend," and likes to have him pay me attention. She worships Ned, & I don't know what she would do if she knew just how far he appreciates having me for his friend.

What is there in me which so attracts men to me, young and old? I am deeply grateful for the power, and I hope I may use it for the good of those who succumb to it; but I really do believe in my heart that it will be many years before Ned gets entirely over it; and I am vain and selfish enough to be glad.

Three weeks later, as Mabel prepared for another Washington trip, she expanded on the situation with Ned and also gave the first definite sign that her husband acquiesced in her flirtations. The passage offers no slightest indication that as Ned's ardor grew, Mabel did anything to discourage him. Blandly she accepted his daily morning visits, remaining unconcerned that his college studies were suffering. During these weeks, as is made clear later in the journal, at Ned's request and while they are in the house together, she sometimes wears his Alpha Delta Phi pin:

> He grows tremendously fonder of me every day. Every morning, regularly, after my first hour of [piano] practice is over he comes in, & he says the whole day goes off exhilaratingly & joyfully after that few moments of talking with me, & perchance touching my hand . . . he says his thoughts are so constantly with me that he cannot think of his recitations, nor in fact of anything else. He takes me to drive regularly twice a week, and would like to every day. . . . It is almost fearful to see his love for me growing so from day to day. I think it is well that I am going away so soon. But I am really very fond of him & I shall miss him very much—& he does not yet begin to realize how much he will miss me. It would be mean and underhanded to write down the tender and loving things he says to me—for they are only for me, & no one else ought to hear them. Of course I tell David in general about it, but my darling husband has perfect trust & confidence in me and tells me to act my own pleasure about these things.

Mabel may have told her husband "in general" about her dalliance with the young son of their good friends, and David may have shown himself up-to-date and open-minded about "these things." But those few words deserve to be highlighted, for they mark the Todds' first steps in what was to prove a steady, at times frightening process of moral disintegration. It would end, years later, with David lamenting that "adultery ruined my life," and adding, in what seems a curious puzzlement, that it was all "like a ghastly dream" (curious, because David's own course as an adulterer was to keep steady pace with his wife's). At the time he made those remarks, in conversation with his own daughter, he was in New York, an inmate of the Bloomingdale Insane Asylum.

Early in April 1882, after having been back in Amherst briefly, Mabel again departed for Washington. Ned also left Amherst that day for a visit to Boston (perhaps only a pretext), and he arranged to accompany Mabel on the train as far as the Palmer Depot interchange. A brief journal entry, made at her parents' home a few days later, shows that during the train ride Mabel had rather enjoyed exercising her "power" over Ned. She had even, it seems, toyed with the idea of an actual indiscretion:

> The dear boy felt more badly about my leaving with every mile. He to all appearances was talking in a lively mood to me on the train, but I could see that he felt dreadfully. I never had a more intense lover, and I don't know what to do about it. . . . Of course I am a woman, and I am older than he, and I know more of life than he, and I can help him somewhat against himself, and I will try. But that is all I can do. Of course, I do care for him—the wonderfully chivalrous devotion he showed me could not fail to affect me—but I love David so wholly that I am not afraid to trust myself entirely to him. . . . I told him that I did care for him, and he said it ought to be enough to make him happy forever.

In Washington the persistent Mr. Elliot resumed his attentions, calling on Mabel regularly. In a journal entry dated May 5 she notes with obvious satisfaction that her friend "walked in the woods with a party of us the other day, & I know that he cares more than ever for me. He longs inexpressibly for love and tenderness, & I am just as sorry for him as I can be."

Expected to attend the Amherst College commencement in early June, as were all the faculty wives, Mabel made a hasty return, planning to stay only a week. She took it for granted that whenever her husband was not available she would be escorted and amused by the adoring Ned. But for once he failed her, and even in the controlled phrasing of the journal her anger at his defection shows plainly:

> I am just now somewhat provoked with Ned, because after telling me that Commencement was nothing to him without me, & that the moment he came in the house he had to find me, & that he was not easy one moment when I was out of his sight, he went off to Pittsfield with a lot of young people just for fun, for a day or two. Of course I do not regard him as my property & bound to entertain me all the time, but it was thoughtless of him to rush off so when I was just leaving his mother for a return to a prosaic boardinghouse, and would be a little blue anyway. But he shall not know I cared in the least, & I don't, except that I should have liked a drive or a horseback ride to cheer me up a little today. He asked me if he should go when the matter was suggested, & I said "by all means," very heartily. . . . I do miss him very much, truly, but I said goodbye radiantly.

After commencement she went back immediately to her parents' Washington home, staying until early August. Except for a brief passage of general remarks on June 30, she did not write in her journal all summer. When next she opened its pages, on September 15, a month after her return to Amherst, the result was another revealing entry, but one in which the interest has suddenly and dramatically shifted: it is no longer young Ned who interests her but his father.

Some rather delicate maneuvering was involved in this deft transfer of attention, and its surface manifestations, at least, may be glimpsed in the many briefer entries Mabel made in her daily diary for those weeks in which she was neglecting her journal. A brief look at the shadowy tale told by the diary, as the summer of 1882 waned in Amherst, will serve as an instructive prelude to the journal entry of mid-September.

Attending lawn teas and musical evenings at the Evergreens, taking part in several outings, Mabel was with the Dickinsons nearly every day from mid-August to early September. The day of her arrival back in Amherst, August 6, she was greeted by Susan, as she noted, "with a most whole-souled 'Welcome home, Toddy,' which was lovely." After an evening of fun at the Evergreens on the thirteenth, Austin walked her home, and he did the same thing again a week later, when Mabel noted in her diary, "I like him immensely." September 6 proved for her quite a busy, not to say demanding, day: she was at the Dickinson house early in the morning and was back again late at night giving, as it seems, equal time to father and son:

> This morning I had a long horseback ride with Ned. We went up on the Leverett road, and after about six miles we stopped under the trees while he smoked. We sat on the fallen leaves & had a pleasant rest. Then we started on again, making at least a ten miles' circuit in all. . . . I went to the Dickinsons' in the evening, & sat alone on the veranda with Mr. Dickinson senior about an hour, discussing religion, thought, & so forth. I admire him.

Next evening she played whist at the Evergreens, with Ned and Mattie. Then on the two following days, September 8 and 9, she once more divided herself between father

and son, and it is here that Ned starts to fade from the
picture.

Twice on the eighth she was in Ned's company, first in the
morning in town, then in the afternoon for a row on the Mill
River. She took supper with the Dickinsons that evening,
and when her husband, after working late, came down to
escort her home he found himself superfluous: "Mr. Dickinson walked home with me, & Ned with David." Next
morning everyone went off in a crowd to spend the day in
the country, and it was while on this outing that Austin—
obviously responding to a signal from Mabel—made his
first overt, if tentative, move in her direction:

> Mr. Dickinson took Grandma & David & Millicent & Gil-
> bert in the carriage to Sugar Loaf. I came later with Ned and
> Mrs. Dickinson & Mattie. Near the foot of the mountain we
> all alighted except Grandma & Millicent. I walked up with
> Mr. Dickinson. He cares a great deal for me. Ned followed
> leading one of the horses.

It was the next day, September 10, that Austin took Mabel
to pay her well-known first visit to the other house. "I sang
there, and the rare, mysterious Emily listened in the quiet
darkness outside," she wrote later in her diary (it is more
probable that the mysterious Emily was upstairs at the
bedside of her invalid mother, while both listened to the
music). After the visit to the Mansion the two returned to
the Evergreens for the evening, and that night both Ned and
his father again walked her home.

Mabel's plans for another sojourn in Washington called
for her to leave Amherst on September 12, so on the day
before she left there was a farewell party at the Dickinsons',
Austin picking her up at the boardinghouse. The two
walked down the hill together, and as they reached the gate

of the Evergreens, Austin made his second move. Before going in to join the others, he suggested, they might take a short stroll, just the two of them. As is made abundantly clear from other records, during that stroll Austin in some way admitted to feeling a very personal and not at all neighborly attraction for his companion. Mabel's response, again according to later records, was prompt and open encouragement of this new suitor, demonstrating not the least concern that he was the husband of her good friend and the father of two youngsters in whose home she frequently found amusement. Next day, even as the Todds prepared to leave, Austin was on hand—in the afternoon he took Mabel off for a carriage ride, and a few hours later saw her to the station.

With so much as background, the journal entry of September 15, made in Washington, will come as less of a surprise:

Everything is so joyous, & my circumstances are so pleasant. And dear Mr. Dickinson—Ned's father—is so very fond of me. It was one of the proudest moments of my life when he told me that I had more ideas which were congenial to him than any other person he ever met. For I most extravagantly admire him. He is in almost every particular my ideal man. He is true—so true that one look into his blue eyes when I first met him caused me to think involuntarily—"He could be forever trusted." I did not really know until lately that he is a very sensitive man, for he has a very strong, almost bluff way with his business relations. But he says he has suffered more than he can ever tell from sensitiveness. . . .

He and I are the fastest friends. To think that out of all the splendid and noble women he has known, he should pick me out—only half his age—as the most truly congenial friend that he had! . . .

The affection I had for Ned is as nothing compared to the strength of interest and admiration I have for his father.

Indeed, Ned & I have tacitly abandoned our little affair, for Ned said it was getting to be with him so strong as to be rapidly getting beyond his control . . . that if he should let go his fierce hold of himself he could not answer for anything. . . . It was a dreadful thing to start up such a fellow as he is, for he has a very strong nature. But as I said everything pales in connection with him beside the glorious character of his father, & his wonderful interest in & affection for me.

A disappointment overtook Mabel in Amherst, in early November, when she was refused permission to accompany her husband on a government astronomical expedition, an exciting event eagerly anticipated. The journal of November 10 shows that when her husband was about taking his departure, she consoled herself with the thought that Austin had given his promise to look after her: "Ned has been very devoted—more so than ever. But my only real joy in staying is because Mr. Dickinson is here, & looks out for me, & has me on his mind. . . . He is delicate beyond expression, and tender & watchful & caretaking." The subject of Austin's tender caretaking she expanded on four days later. Almost incidentally she also records the fact that, at last, the sensitive father had wholly supplanted the callow son:

I am not alone very much, for everyone is very kind to me, especially the Dickinsons, & of them especially Mr. Dickinson. Mattie & Ned are very bright and brilliant, but being so very young are much on the surface. . . . To be sure Ned was very much in love with me once, and would say and do all sorts of things to & for me now, if I were a particle responsive. . . . I really did care for him a great deal, in one way, some time ago, but I have not a particle of that romantic interest in him left. The point where, if he had known it, he could have made me have a very permanent and deep affection for him is passed long by, and I am delighted to see how entirely he has passed out of my life. . . . It was in the middle of last summer that I decided to give Ned nothing more in the way of my regard, so I put him out. About that time, or, no, somewhat later, his father and I began to discover that we had a great many ideas in common, and from that began a friendship which is the most true and satisfying that I ever had. He thoroughly appreciates and understands me, and nothing is too subtle and delicate for him to see. The way in which he cares for me & looks out for my comfort & happiness is beyond expression.

Telling its own curious tale, of course, is the afterthought in that passage ("or, no, somewhat later"). With that disingenuous phrase Mabel actually tries to make it appear that before settling her affections on the father, she had completely finished with the son. But the attempt, of course, is belied by her own previous journal entries. Here, strangely, she has told a barefaced lie to herself.

As the year 1882 ran out, the friendship with Austin had become "my chief joy," and Austin himself "the most true and satisfying friend I ever had. I respect and admire him boundlessly. I wish I could write of it but it is beyond writing." Even as she exults (yet again) in her happy and accomplished and "brilliant" life, she indulges in a curious, and sadly prophetic, linkage of Austin and her husband: "David has had exceptional success & is coming to me within a few days—and my admirable, noble, strong, true Mr. Dickinson is entirely devoted to me."

Before she could make another journal entry, the January 1883 trouble with the jealous Sue erupted. While that initial unpleasantness was fairly soon calmed by the "frank" talk between the two women, bad feeling broke out again several weeks later. The following journal passage was written by Mabel on February 3, within days after the

second outbreak. It is a crucial entry and requires careful
reading, for Mabel, far from setting down objective truth,
is seeking to excuse her own conduct. Whatever it was
exactly that the idealistic Ned chanced to see going on
between his father and Mabel—certainly more than walks
and rides—it was enough to disgust as well as thoroughly
disillusion him:

> I am not very happy just at present . . . the root of all my
> trouble is that I allowed that affair with Ned to progress too
> much. I got over all especial feeling for him in the summer,
> and supposed he did for me. . . . But he is of a very jealous
> disposition, & began to think I must care more for his father
> than himself. So he got angry and went to his mother with
> some very mean things—among other things telling her that
> I was an awful flirt, & having allowed him to fall in love with
> me, I was now tired of him & was trying the same thing with
> his father. Of course this troubled her very much, & she
> began to look about. . . .
>   Ned is excessively polite to me, but I am angry enough for
> anything with him—and I am so sorry for it all. As for his
> father he is as staunch & true as still [*sic*] to me—but I do not
> see him except very rarely. It is better not, I suppose. But I
> like him just as much as ever, & he does me. Of that I am
> absolutely sure.

When she made her next entry, dated April 10, 1883,
Mabel was again in Washington, and David had once more
left home on business. Emily and Vinnie had both by now
entered the fray on their brother's behalf—Emily with her
two notes, Vinnie in person—hoping to placate the angry
Susan and restore family harmony. The information Mabel
now set down about the marriage of Austin and Susan was
supposedly told her in the preceding two months by Austin

himself. Her daily diary does show that the two were together on a dozen occasions during that period, including five times when they walked or rode alone, allowing ample opportunity for the sort of intimate talk reflected in the journal. But, again, the charges Mabel makes here must be read with caution—or better, must be read in a mood of high skepticism. Consciously or otherwise, she has certainly both exaggerated and distorted whatever it was that Austin told her. Austin himself in such a situation scarcely provides disinterested testimony.

> David started this morning. I felt terribly to leave him. We have been so much to each other since our separation last fall, while he was in California, that it seemed to me I could not let him go. We have been together constantly, & the companionship is inexpressibly sweet.
>
> Mr. Dickinson has told me a great many things since I last wrote, and he is more absorbed in me than I can write. It seems he & his wife have not been in the least happy together, although for the sake of appearances, & for the children, they have continued to live together. Notwithstanding the utter lack of love between them, the fact that he is so interested in me has stirred her beyond the power of words to express. And she makes it pretty dreadful for him at home. I have seen some developments in her character which are very startling. But I do admire her in most respects very much. We have courteous relations, but that is all. This whole thing has weighed my spirits down dreadfully—it is the cause of my languor and weakness & lack of enthusiasm. There are aspects of it which hurt me terribly. Aside from that, everything is joyous—except my darling David going away today. I have nearly wept my eyes out over that.
>
> Mr. Dickinson's life has been very barren, & I understand him thoroughly. He is the rarest nature I have ever met. Honor & purity & pathos & strength. And it has come to mean all the world to him—his feeling for me.

That Austin did in some manner complain to Mabel about one or another aspect of his home life, whether or not justified, is probable. That he used such phrases as "not in the least happy" and "utter lack of love," or that he claimed he had stayed with Susan for the children's sake, are things quite improbable. Such a serious estrangement—given what is known of the Dickinsons' twenty-five years together before Mabel's arrival on the scene—simply lacks all support. Further, the unnamed but ominous-sounding "developments" in Sue's character, considering the manner in which her wayward husband was behaving, could not have been so startling as all that. It would have been much more startling—and infinitely more revealing—had Susan failed to show some fire.

With David out of town, Mabel and Austin now went a step further as they proceeded to make plans for a rendezvous out from under the knowing eyes of Amherst. It was to take place in Boston in the summer, she coming down from her vacation resort in New Hampshire, supposedly for a day of shopping, he going up from Amherst. Their meeting place was the horsecar stop on Winter Street, the date June 30. As arranged, the tryst came off smoothly, the two not parting until late evening, when Mabel, as she wrote in her journal, "went back to Winchester on wings as it were." Less than two weeks later Austin wrote his first private note to Mabel of definite date, and it shows that Susan had not been fooled by her husband's Boston excursion. It also shows that Austin, like the good lawyer he was, had his defense prepared—a straightforward claim, of the Sam Bowles variety, that he had nothing to hide in arranging to meet a friend in another town, even if that friend happened to be an attractive young married woman. The session with Sue he describes took place the day after his arrival back home from Boston:

At breakfast next morning the question came square—after leading up properly—"Did you see Mrs. Todd?" I had anticipated it and said at once, "Certainly, that was what I went to Boston for." This unhesitating frankness was somewhat stunning and the rally wasn't prompt. When it came it was, "She told me she was to spend a few days in Boston before going to Hampton and I concluded you would see her." I replied yes I *said* I did. This ended it. There has been no allusion to it, or you, since. I don't know whether on the whole I am supposed to have lied about it or not, but *you* know I spoke the truth.

Surprisingly, Austin's bold tactic worked, to an extent at least, and by the date of this letter, July 12, 1883, matters at the Evergreens had more or less settled down again. For the remaining days of July it was decided that Austin would join his family, evenings after work, at a holiday spot in nearby Shutesbury, returning to town each morning. With that, Vinnie and Emily, watching anxiously from next door, must have concluded with relief and no little satisfaction that peace had at last been restored or was on its way. In the minds of all concerned the summer months of 1883 began to drift by at their old, serene pace.

But once again the aura of peace was woefully deceptive. An unusually long, frank, and introspective journal entry Mabel made in mid-September at Hampton, her first in more than four months, warns only of a rapidly gathering storm. Its opening paragraph introduces still another Washington admirer, one who briefly rivaled the romantic Mr. Elliot:

I remained in Washington until about the middle of May, having a very brilliant time, as I always do there. Dr. Eaton was especially devoted to me. But I have had all the experience I ever want with jealous wives, so I did not let it progress very much. . . .

[In Amherst in June] Mrs. Dickinson was still very chaotic and not sweet. Another unfortunate incident occurred which irritated her. So beyond a call or two exchanged, where everything was courteous, we had no relations. Mr. D. kept me perfectly informed of every aspect of her mind, and everything she said, and was himself marvelously thoughtful and tender to me. Fifty little kindnesses & more he poured upon me. He is the truest and most loyally affectionate of men. But he has had a wretched life at home, in spite of the perfect house & grounds, the carriages & horses, the pictures & luxuries generally. He is equally lovely to David, and the sweet and trusting relationship between us three is one of the most beautiful things that ever came into my life—to say nothing of the rest of it. . . .

[David] has been so tender & thoughtful of me through my sadness owing to Mrs. Dickinson and Ned, and has constantly devised so many little diversions and pleasures, that I should be indeed most ungrateful if I did not respond & show forth my shining blue sky again. And I do—my happiness has come back again. With two such rare men to do for me, & to hold my happiness above everything in their lives, how could I be sad! . . .

Mrs. D. is so well understood there that the fact of her breaking with us [the previous spring] cannot redound to her credit. I have never spoken about it to anyone, but a lady said to me that it was a matter of wonder with my friends that there had been no break before. It was Mrs. D's way to have some "fuss" on hand most of the time. Notwithstanding all that I hear about her, I do admire her mind. And she stimulates me intellectually. And I cannot blame her for her frantic efforts to regain the respect & love of her husband—which she has not had for more than twenty years. She has tried in every way, and she cannot move him—coldness, hauteur, affectionateness, commanding, indignation—nothing succeeds. And now she sees that he is immovable, that his affection for David and myself is permanent, and she can do nothing more. So she yields gracefully & takes us in partially again. But she will not wish him to see much of me.

Mr. D. says she fears me—the first woman who has really crossed her path—fears me because she *knows* I have stirred him as no other woman has *ever* stirred him. Though she has gone her own way all these years, and has never tried to keep him, doing all the time things morally certain to do more than alienate him from her—yet now when she sees that he has turned to me, & finds peace & content & congeniality in being with me, she chafes & raves & cannot endure it. The greatest joy in life lay beside her for years, & she never moved to retain it, even pushed it from her. Now it has left her irrevocably, & she sees the awful loss & void. She has the husk from which the soul is departed. And I cannot blame her, nor do other than deeply pity her.

But when I see the holy joy rise in his eyes when he sees me, and the youthful beauty glow over his face, and contrast it with the apathetic, careless indifference which was his leading characteristic for months after we first knew him, I cannot but rejoice for the happiness I have brought him. For the first time in his life he lives, he says. And I admire him & respect him & love him. So David does also. . . .

Yes, oh! yes, life is full of joy & sweetness. The sun shines, the dear crickets chirp, the red leaves flutter down, the sparkling sea sings to me. People love me—books, music, painting minister to me, and I love it all so deeply!

Crying out for prompt comment is that admiring compliment to herself that Mabel puts into Austin's mouth, the statement that "for the first time in his life he lives." If Austin really did say that, or anything like it, and said it in full awareness, then he stands convicted not only of insincerity but of the classic male ploy in such affairs. The many fervent letters he wrote to Susan during their courtship thirty years before, all of them at that moment reposing in the attic of the Evergreens, pour out his romantic feelings in precisely the same hurried, overblown style as anything he was to pen later to Mabel. The only difference detectable between earlier and later love letters is of the sort to be expected from the span of years, and from the fact that the youthful ones were written with marriage in mind.

While a few select portions of this outspoken entry have been quoted and commented on before, its deeper implications have managed to elude notice. There is, to start with, the rather chilling self-indulgence of Mabel's pleasure in having "two such rare men to do for me, & to hold my happiness above everything in their lives." Here she proclaims that in her own eyes at any rate, her conquest of Austin is more or less complete, nor does she give any thought to the harm her victory may do others, notably the three Dickinson children. Equally disturbing is her remark about Sue being "well understood" in Amherst society. The real thrust of this statement, in its own subtle way not a little shocking, does much to fix the truth of Mabel's underlying character. Here she expresses a confident hope that Sue's *prior* reputation in town for personal embroilment will now happily prove useful to her, supplying a cover for her own budding affair with Austin. Any disturbance that might be created by the wronged wife, in other words, will be put down among townspeople to Mrs. Dickinson's supposed prickly temper, her liking for a fuss, leaving Mabel unscathed and unsuspected.

The other charges leveled at Sue in that passage—principally blaming her for a supposed two-decade crumbling of her marriage—on the available evidence may, again, be dismissed. No doubt over the years the marriage had known its share of rough times, and perhaps by the eighties affection on one side or the other had worn thin, waxing and waning, like most. But it was not any noticeable strain in his homelife that had produced Austin's "apathetic" air. The real cause was something even sadder, that same oppressive burden that so often weighs down a certain kind of man as he reaches his mid-fifties, an awful sense of having fallen short. When Mabel came to know him, the talented, ambitious Austin had already begun to feel an almost panic sense of failure, a conviction that the grand promise of his youth would not be realized. More than any temporary disappointments as husband and father, what finally made him want to stray from his marriage vows was bitter regret over all his broken dreams of success, as he put it, among "men of the world and affairs" in the larger sphere beyond Amherst.

That is a dangerous mood to lay hold of any man. All too often his resentment, smoldering beneath the indifference, prepares him to fall a ready victim to circumstance. At that moment, in the early fall of 1883, fate had in store for Austin, and for all the Dickinson clan, one last, truly devastating circumstance, the death of little Gilbert.

3

My Ascended Playmate

WITH HER BROTHER'S personal and family troubles seemingly under control in the late spring of 1883, Emily was free to turn her full attention to two unlooked-for but supremely exciting developments in her own life. Against all probability, it now began to appear that her old, earnest hopes for fulfillment, as both woman and artist, might after all be realized. The poetry, at least some of it, could well see publication, and not in the ephemeral pages of newspapers and magazines but in book form. Even more wonderful, the reclusive life itself might finally have an end, since Judge Lord, making an astonishing recovery from the stroke that had felled him the year before, was again talking in his determined fashion of a wedding. The reality of both these developments has been much debated, but to many minds the evidence in their favor is sufficient, and it clearly shows Emily responding in grateful acceptance of her double resurrection. A decade and a half of confinement to the rooms, halls, and stairways of her father's house had not robbed her of either the ability or the desire to touch, and be touched by, the world beyond.

Just why Emily, in the first instance, gave up trying to

achieve publication is an endlessly tantalizing question, one often asked but which seems doomed to continue unanswered, at any rate to general satisfaction. That she did in fact make such a conscious decision is certain. The time of the decision is also fairly definite, and may be referred to the period of the Civil War, or just after, when she had on hand some thousand brief poems, of which perhaps half merited publication. During her final twenty years, in other words, while she continued to write at the rate of about thirty poems annually (of course, all quite brief), she made no further attempt to find a publisher. Whether her original decision to withhold her work was seen by her as permanent is beyond knowing, and perhaps Emily herself would have admitted to uncertainty on the point. In any case, her resolve not to publish had already begun to waver in April 1882, when she found herself reading an unexpected invitation from a well-known Boston publisher whose interest had been stimulated by one of its authors, Helen Hunt Jackson: " 'H. H.' once told me that she wished you could be induced to publish a volume of poems. I should not want to say how highly she praised them, but to such an extent that I wish also that you could."

That a word of praise from Mrs. Jackson, then America's best-known woman writer, who had read perhaps a hundred of Emily's poems in manuscript (those in the possession of her friend T. W. Higginson, as well as the few Emily sent directly to her), should have been enough to draw an outright invitation from the respected firm of Roberts Brothers is not surprising. Of much greater import is the nature of Emily's reply, which shows her, even if hesitantly, starting to reconsider her decision not to publish. "The kind but incredible opinion of 'H. H.' and yourself I would like to deserve," she answered Thomas Niles, head of Roberts Brothers, enclosing a poem. "Would you accept a Pebble I think I gave to her, though I am not sure." *I would like to deserve*: those few words, consciously and deliberately addressed to a man whose business it was to evaluate and publish all kinds of writing, can only mean that Emily was looking with favor on the proposal.

Some cloudy circumstance, now indeterminable, interrupted the exchange at that point, and it was almost exactly a year later when the correspondence was resumed. In fact, it was Emily herself who initiated this second stage, in March 1883, when she wrote to ask Niles about a forthcoming biography of George Eliot (information she could have found more quickly much closer to home). Niles responded by sending Emily a gift copy of a new Eliot biography by another author, and she in turn sent him her personal copy of the Brontë sisters' *Poems* of 1847. With it she enclosed two of her own verses, taking the unusual action, for her, of titling both. "My Cricket" and "The Snow," she called them.

Niles, not wanting to accept so rare a volume as the Brontë, returned it, and in so doing took the opportunity to renew his offer of the previous year, but couched in terms even more emphatic: "If I may presume to say so, I will take instead a MS. collection of your poems, that is, if you want to give them to the world through the medium of a publisher." The intervening months had done nothing to lessen Niles's hopes of discovering a new author, and it may be that he had seen still others of Emily's poems, through Mrs. Jackson or Higginson, or had heard something about her through someone else. Emily's response this time, still a bit coy, was to send three poems, including the fine "No Brigadier throughout the year," which she titled "The Bird." When Niles a few days later wrote that he especially liked "The Bird," she promptly sent him three more poems, again giving them titles: "Country Burial," "The Humming Bird," and "Thunderstorm." Niles replied with a simple thank-you and his assurances that he had read all the poems with "great pleasure." In his professional way he was saying that he would await further shipments of manuscript, if that was how Emily preferred to do it, hoping eventually to have enough for a volume.

Niles now had in his personal possession the manuscripts of at least ten of Emily's poems, all of them among her best, and it is very likely that he had read many others. That he failed to pursue so promising an author more aggressively is unfortunate, but his leisurely approach does not, as is claimed, argue a slackening of interest. Like any leading publisher, then or now, he could not envision a serious writer, particularly an unknown, actually hesitating over, or declining, what amounted to a serious offer. Why Emily herself held back in the face of Niles's invitation, as it appears she did, to an extent, is a more pertinent question. All that can be suggested in that regard, however, concerns one overlooked fact: it was now, the late spring of 1883, that Emily was caught up in the troubles erupting next door. Her two veiled notes of friendly reprimand, one to Sue and the other to Mabel, according to careful reckoning were sent sometime in May, perhaps early June. It would have been summer's end—when Sue generously admitted to being "wrong" about Mabel—before a calmer Emily might have decided to do something about Niles's offer. The task of selecting several dozen poems for a volume, out of the seventeen hundred she had on hand, could not have been a simple one and might easily have consumed weeks or months, taking her into the fall.

Similarly traceable—admittedly by means of evidence largely circumstantial—are her renewed hopes of marriage with Judge Lord. As is now well understood, Lord and Emily had known, and been attracted to, each other for many years before the late blossoming of their romance. It is not improbable, in fact, that Lord was the mysterious "Master" of Emily's middle years, the married man with whom she was so desperately and hopelessly in love. In any case, it was not long after the death of Mrs. Lord in December 1877 that Emily and the judge—now referring to each other in correspondence as "Mama" and "Papa"—began thinking seriously of marriage. Various unavoidable family matters on both sides combined to delay the event (the paralysis of the elderly Mrs. Dickinson, for one, followed by Emily's understandable reluctance to leave her sister alone). Still, had it not been for the stroke suffered by Lord early in 1882, it is nearly certain that Emily would have ended her life not as a village eccentric but as proud mistress of her own home and servants in Lord's hometown of Salem. (Strangely, this picture of Emily released from her long imprisonment and returned to normal life, whether still writing poetry or not, is actually displeasing to many of her present-day admirers. Much of the reluctance to credit the possibility of a marriage to Lord, both before and after the stroke of 1882, may be laid to this attitude. How unwarrantedly intrusive, sometimes, is the literary imagination upon the sober reality of everyday things!)

For the indomitable Lord, as it turned out, the stroke proved a mere temporary setback. By year's end he had nearly, or quite, recovered, and it was at that time, November 1882, that Emily penned the well-known passage in a letter to Lord in which she makes herself his wife by anticipation: "Emily Jumbo! Sweetest name, but I know a sweeter—Emily Jumbo Lord. Have I your approval?" (Much in the public eye just then was Barnum's great elephant attraction, the famous Jumbo, and Lord in some joking manner must have applied the name to Emily.) A second letter from Emily to Lord, written soon after, shows that she had even consented to the unusual step of leaving her home and traveling up to Salem to visit him, probably for the Christmas 1882 holidays. "You said with loved timidity in asking me to your dear Home," she wrote, "you would 'try not to make it unpleasant.' . . . You even call me to your breast with apology! . . . the tender Priest of Hope need not allure his Offering—'Tis on his altar ere he asks." Not to be overlooked in that passage is the implied meaning—when read in the context of an impending marriage—of that unusual phrase *Priest of Hope*.

Whether Emily actually made the journey to Salem at Christmas that year cannot be said, though it is not really so improbable a step as many seem to think. But that Lord came down to see her in Amherst the next year is a fact. On September 8, 1883, accompanied by the several close relatives with whom he made his home in Salem, he arrived in town and put up at the Amherst Hotel. The visit lasted at least four days, and on three occasions Lord called at the Evergreens, certainly each time going next door. Still surviving are several short notes written to him by Emily while he was in town, and they preserve undisguised sentiments of loving intimacy. "I feel like wasting my Cheek on your Hand tonight," she confided in one note, "will you accept the squander?" When Lord and his party left Amherst for the return home, her farewell note included a subtle reminder of their hours together: "The withdrawal of the Fuel of Rapture does not withdraw the Rapture itself."

Perhaps it may now be agreed that by mid-September 1883, as all the above facts proclaim, the two separate but converging strands that made up Emily Dickinson's hopes for happiness in what was left to her of this life had come thrillingly together—miraculously, as it must have seemed to her then. After thirty years of yearning, after suffering through long periods of alternating hope and despair, she

was at last to possess what she had always wanted. Simultaneously she would become both a wife and a recognized
poet.

★   ★   ★

BY THE TIME Gilbert Dickinson turned eight years old, on
August 1, 1883, he had already established himself as a
favorite of his neighbors in north Amherst. He was an
active, spirited child, gregarious of temperament, and people often smiled at the stories that went around about him.
One in particular told at this time concerned his being stung
by a bee—as his mother was trying to comfort him,
through tear-filled eyes he insisted, quite seriously it is said,
that the offending insects be read to from the Bible. As if in
support of that little story his aunt Emily recorded the
child's understandable preoccupation thereafter with bees.
"There's sumthn else—there's Bumbul Beese," she reported him interjecting into any and all conversations of the
grown-ups in his hearing.

Emily was also quite impressed, it appears, with Gib's
budding skill in language, to be seen in his readiness to
bestow distinctive names on any local character who caught
his fancy. "The Cloudy Man," he dubbed a Negro laborer,
and an acquaintance newly married became "Mister Bridegroom." When the boy was six, Emily preserved one of his
slyly evocative remarks in a note sent across the lawn to his
mother: "Memoirs of little boys that live—'Weren't you
chasing Pussy,' said Vinnie to Gilbert? 'No—she was chasing herself'—'But wasn't she running pretty fast?'—'Well,
some slow and some fast' said the beguiling villain." That
such close attention paid to the doings and sayings of an
eight-year-old boy was not wholly a result of family pride
may be seen in a note of Gib's, the only one of his childish
letters to have survived. It was sent to a playmate two days

after Christmas 1882, when he was seven and a half. The handwriting is sprawling, but the spelling is precise, and the earnest concern about his sister, seven years older, by all accounts was typical: "My Dear Sally I thought I would write and thank you for the very pretty book you sent me. last night I wrot to Ned and told him that Matty had decided to go to Pittsfield I told him to take care of her if he would I said I would be very much obliged if he would. I had seven books and seven cards and I had a canon that would shoot nine pins Christmas and I had battle dore and shutelcock. So good by your friend Gilbert."

The boy's innocent appeal was not simply a matter of parental indulgence, for in the fashion of the day he was encouraged to conduct himself rather as a smaller version of the much older Ned. A neighbor living across Main Street from the Evergreens frequently saw the two Dickinson boys leave the house on their way to Sunday services, and on one occasion she described them in a letter: Ned, proper with cane and beaver hat, and Gib walking along beside him "with *his* little cane as dignified as his brother."

Aside from a nasty fall backward out of a bouncing carriage, there is no record of Gib's having suffered any very serious accident or illness through his first eight years. He was considered a healthy child, so when he came down with a slight fever two weeks after the start of school in the autumn of 1883, there was no great concern, though he was kept home and put to bed. Next day, Saturday, September 29, he was a little worse, and when evening brought a hailstorm, accompanied by thunder and lightning, Sue and Austin took turns comforting him through the night. Sunday he rested easy in bed, on Monday seemed to be improving, and by Tuesday it was cautiously decided that he was on the mend. Next morning he suffered a slight relapse, however, and it was at that point that the doctor rendered his frightening diagnosis: typhoid. Inquiries in the neighborhood established that on the previous Thursday he had been playing with a friend in a nearby mudhole. Though the playmate—Kendall Emerson, son of the geology professor at Amherst College and a good friend of the Dickinsons—had not been affected, it was decided that water in the hole had been the source of the disease.

Alarm spread quickly through both houses, and though she was still recovering from an ankle sprain, Emily hastened across the lawn to be with her nephew. During the agonizing crisis of the next three days she spent more time at her brother's house, hovering with everyone else near the sickbed, than at her own. That fact may seem too obvious to warrant specific mention, but it is made with a purpose. Those more informed will notice that it contradicts one of the accepted beliefs of Emily's life: that for her last fifteen years she never set foot inside the Evergreens except briefly on the night Gib died. But that assertion rests on the offhand statement of a single neighbor, one not intimate with the Dickinsons and who in fact never met Emily. Even if the evidence were much stronger than that, it would fail to convince many that during the eight interminable days of her nephew's illness Emily never crossed the lawn to be with him.

Through Wednesday, October 3, the boy continued to sink, and late on the fourth it was recognized that he had reached the crisis. All through that night the lights at the Evergreens burned brightly, and by three in the morning Emily had reached the limit of her endurance. Physically unable to stand the ordeal any longer, her condition made worse by the astringent odors of the medicines and disinfectants in the sickroom, with a raging headache she was taken back to the Mansion, where she vomited violently and was put to bed.

On the morning of the fifth, after a "dreadful night," Gib's condition grew rapidly worse. Emily, still weak from the night before, returned to the boy's bedside and was there when he became delirious. Later she reported what may have been his last words: trying to sit up, he began calling out, "Open the door, open the door, they are waiting for me!" When she wrote down that pathetic cry some weeks later she added, "*Who* were waiting for him, all we possess we would give to know." Through the long afternoon the decline in respiration went inexorably on. It was fifteen minutes before five o'clock when little Gib Dickinson stopped breathing.

Mabel Todd had returned to Amherst from the Hamptons on September 29, just in time to share in the initial anxiety over Gib's illness. During the week of the brutal siege she stayed away from the Evergreens, obtaining news of the boy through Vinnie. Only on the morning of the fifth did she venture as far as the Dickinsons' door, where Mattie explained the extreme seriousness of Gib's condition. That evening, returning from a carriage ride with her husband, she heard the news of the boy's death. "My heart is breaking for his father," she wrote in her diary that night. "Oh! the dear man, how he is suffering." When she called at the Mansion next morning, she was told by Vinnie—herself near prostration—that Austin "looked like death, but is calmer than she feared." For what it is worth, a curious fact may be noted here: nowhere in her diaries, journals, or letters, at the time or afterward, did Mabel have anything whatever to say about the dead little boy himself or about her own feelings at the tragedy of his loss.

The funeral was held on Monday, October 8, at three in the afternoon. It was conducted by the Dickinsons' old friend, Reverend Jonathan Jenkins, formerly of Amherst, whose children had often played with Gib and who came over from Pittsfield to be on hand. Also attending, besides many of the immediate neighbors, were Mabel and her husband, as well as Maria Whitney, friend of both Emily and her brother, and the son of Sam Bowles, up from Springfield. Sue could not face accompanying the coffin to the cemetery, so when the funeral carriages moved from the church out to the street she sought seclusion across the way at the Evergreens, where a kindly neighbor remained with her and kept the parlor fire going. Emily went neither to church nor to cemetery, apparently, though from the east window of her upstairs bedroom she would have had the church in full sight. From another window she could have watched the funeral procession as it passed along Main Street in front of the Mansion, then turned north into Triangle Road.

Sue's sister Martha, living in Geneva, New York, a woman who some years earlier had had to bear a similar loss, sent within a day or two a note of sympathy which may stand as a symbol or echo of the anguished grief that now settled over both houses: "God help all you poor brokenhearted ones—I can only love you and grieve with you my dearest sister . . . you have not a thought that I do not understand, nor a pain—Oh the mystery and horror of it all—Poor Austin—What can I do for you now or ever? . . . you will tell me if you want me—I think of you every moment—Life seems so hard but Oh so short."

The younger Bowles, who had not been to Amherst for some time before his attendance at the funeral, also wrote a friend of his sorrow, recalling the lost little boy of whom he had been so fond: "I can still hear him calling me with a pretty lisp 'Misther Sam'! Last Christmas I sent him as usual a little gift and then for the first time he wrote me himself a cunning note in acknowledgement. And now the little chap is no longer alive to greet me when I go to Amherst."

The fine obituary of Gib that was printed twelve days later in the *Amherst Record* was written by some Amherst acquaintance of the family, strangely never identified, who had been able to observe Gib at close quarters. It is not often that so young a child manages to make such a strong and clear impression as is sketched out here:

Death of a Promising Boy

Gilbert Dickinson, youngest son of Wm. A. Dickinson, died on the afternoon of Friday, October 5th, after a very short but severe attack of fever. He was at school on Thursday of the week before. He was only eight years old and yet we are astonished to find how many Gilbert interested. . . . People not only played with him to see the child-life show itself, but they talked with him for their own pleasure.

When the village heard of his death we felt as if one had gone who had established a place for himself among us. We loved him as one in whom the qualities that men "tie to" were freshened by the dew of childhood. Nor did this lessen his hearty enjoyment of all that children delight in. He was a real child only his interests were very broad for such a little fellow. As if by intuition, he found the real stuff of humanity beneath all sorts of garbs and in persons old as well as young. . . .

That he liked a person was enough. Whatever others might think of his friends he was always loyal. He liked so many that he took it for granted that many liked him, and when he stopped an older person in the street to see him ride his velocipede it was not because he thought he rode better than other boys but because of a common interest he supposed people had in each other. . . .

But his affection was not less intense because it was broad. At times he could not bear to see even the picture of one of his little friends who had left town. It must be turned to the wall. And this wide and intense affection found abundant, even

delicious expression in his words to those he loved. . . .
Hopes are always buried with children but not often do we
lose in the death of so young a boy so much of actual fruition.
He not only promised much but already had provided much.

Wrung out by her grief, Emily was able to find solace,
curiously enough, only in a note of sympathy sent by a
minister who had served at the Dickinsons' church. The
thought it conveyed was of the simplest, suggesting that
Gib's passing was part of God's plan: "I can but believe that
in such a mysterious providence as the dying of little Gilbert there is a purpose of benevolence which does not
include our present happiness." Those words Emily later
recalled as "our only spar" in the first days of biting sorrow, and it was from them, perhaps, that she drew strength
to reach a hand of comfort toward her stricken sister-in-
law. The first note she sent across the lawn, evidently
written within days of the funeral, accompanied flowers
and was wisely kept short: "Perhaps the dear, grieved heart
would open to a flower, which blesses unrequested, and
serves without a sound."

Her second note was much longer, and was obviously
composed with great care, moving no doubt through several drafts. In its incandescent evoking of the departed boy's
radiant spirit, and especially its high literary finish, it
strikingly reveals Emily attempting to find rest for her own
agitated heart, as well as soothe that of the boy's mother. Its
five brief paragraphs, mounting steadily to a climax like
stanzas in a poem, focus on different aspects of the same
idea. The fact that she took the trouble to write at all—to a
recipient a few feet away—shows how much she had come
to depend on the written rather than the spoken word for
the expression of her deepest feelings:

DEAR SUE—

The Vision of Immortal Life has been fulfilled—How simply at the last the Fathom comes! The Passenger and not the Sea, we find surprises us—

Gilbert rejoiced in Secrets—His life was panting with them—With what menace of Light he cried "Don't tell Aunt Emily!" Now my ascended Playmate must instruct *me*. Show us, prattling Preceptor, but the way to thee!

He knew no niggard moment—His life was full of boon— The Playthings of the Dervish were not so wild as his—No crescent was this creature—He traveled from the Full—Such soar, but never set—

I see him in the Star, and meet his sweet velocity in everything that flies—His life was like the Bugle, which winds itself away, his Elegy an echo—His Requiem ecstacy— Dawn and Meridian in one.

Wherefore would he wait, wronged only of Night, which he left for us—Without a speculation, our little Ajax spans the whole—

> Pass to thy rendezvous of Light,
> Pangless except for us—
> Who slowly ford the mystery
> Which thou hast leaped across!

EMILY.

In the main, that closing quatrain accomplishes two things. First, it offers for solace the one thought that has proven power in such sorrow, the idea that the living will sooner or later rejoin those who have departed ("He is only on the road ahead of us," Leigh Hunt wrote of the dead Keats, "and we will soon catch up"). Second, it wonderfully enforces the feeling of continuity between this life and the afterlife, death becoming only a door to be opened or a stream to be forded. The same thing, and even more effectively, had earlier been done by Emily in what is probably her finest poem, "Because I could not stop for death."

A third note she wrote Sue is more practical, reminding the heartbroken mother that even the most awful pain will have an end: "Hopelessness in its first Film has not leave to last. That would close the Spirit, and no intercession could do that. Intimacy with Mystery, after great space, will usurp its place." If similar notes went to her brother, none has survived. In any case, both father and mother continued through the next month to suffer the weight of that inevitable crushed and empty feeling, and neither was seen much if at all outside the house. Sue, fearing, as she said, that she would "break down" if she met anyone beyond her own family, remained secluded indoors, receiving only one or two of her closest neighbors. For Austin in that same period there is only a single indication of his state, and again it is a comment supplied by Mabel Todd, a strangely superficial comment, as it would prove. On the afternoon of October 13, while Mabel was visiting Vinnie at the Mansion, Austin walked in. The two went off by themselves to the quiet of the veranda where they had a long talk. "He seems entirely himself," Mabel noted that night in her diary, "though sad of course. He is a magnificent man."

A more experienced observer than Mabel might have noticed more, or might have guessed the truth, that Austin's placid demeanor that afternoon was highly deceptive. As she and everyone else shortly learned, Austin's grief over the loss of his little son was of that "perfect" kind, so well described by his poet sister as "passionless," and it had already begun to work in him some profound changes. He had twelve more years to live, but never again would he be entirely himself, a fact that his daughter in her maturity, looking back on these pathetic days, would take the trouble to emphasize:

> After Gilbert's death nothing was ever the same in either household. Emily's "impregnable chances" of life were no longer impregnable. Nothing was sure. Nothing was as it had been—or as it would have been in the future had he lived. . . . Austin's life had received new revelation in the little son of his maturity, that was almost rebirth. He never gathered his shattered world together again in its first triumphal pattern.

No one, then, was aware of it, or could have been, but Martha's threefold repetition of the word *nothing* in that passage had its own subtle purpose. She was putting on record the firm belief of her mother and herself that what happened next, Austin's defection to the arms of Mabel Todd while publicly retaining his place at the head of the Dickinson household, grew directly out of the untimely and devastating loss of his son: "Nothing was ever the same. . . . Nothing was sure. Nothing was as it had been."

★   ★   ★

THE SHUDDERING BLOW dealt Emily by her nephew's death, besides sending her back to her bed with what the doctors were to call "revenge of the nerves," was also the likely cause of the more serious condition that now began to take her in its deadly grip: overwhelming emotional strain, where there is a predisposition, is often the precipitant of Bright's disease (technically nephritis, or kidney malfunction).

For the remainder of that year she was confined to bed under a doctor's care, though there was little, aside from bed rest and restriction of liquids, that could be done then in treating the illness. The day of pharmaceutical specifics had not yet dawned, and only a few simple medicines were available, mostly narcotics in dilution, and an array of innocuous salts and syrups. All of these, as is shown by the many surviving prescriptions, were regularly administered to Emily, of course with small benefit. Before she was allowed up again it was late February 1884, and her activities were restricted to giving light assistance in the work of the kitchen. "I shall make Wine Jelly tonight," she wrote a friend about now, happy to be up again, "and send you a Tumbler."

With her health slowly improving, and the pain of Gib's loss at least a little dulled, her thoughts gradually came back to everyday matters and in the process could hardly have avoided the subject of marriage with Judge Lord. If there was any slight hope of a union remaining at this time, it was suddenly and cruelly crushed once more, this time permanently. On March 11, 1884, Judge Lord in Salem was felled by another massive stroke. For two days he lingered, and then, as Emily herself later described it, "After a brief unconsciousness, a Sleep that ended with a smile, so his nieces tell us, he hastened away." With that second loss she seems to have ceased caring much about anything, including the interest of Roberts Brothers in her poetry. Even if she had wished to pursue the contact already established with the receptive Thomas Niles, it was too late, for her own health now gave way. Twice during the remaining months of 1884 she was to be struck down by the increasing malignancy coursing through her veins.

In mid-June, while she was engaged in baking, she blacked out and fell to the kitchen floor. When she awoke in bed late that night, after some ten hours in a coma, she thought she was dying, as indeed did her hovering family.

As was to be expected, her recovery was slow, and the remainder of the summer she spent convalescing in bed or sitting wrapped in a chair in her room. The second incident occurred that October, while she was alone in the parlor. As before, with little or no warning she fainted and lay for some two hours undiscovered on the floor. It was Vinnie who found her, almost at the same moment as her brother, who had dropped in from next door. As her family must have guessed, it was the beginning of the end. From this time on, a matter of eighteen months, Emily was to live as an invalid, never or seldom straying from the confines of her second-floor bedroom. Her time was spent in reading, some books, but mostly the lighter fare of magazines and newspapers, and writing an occasional letter. She did continue writing verse, but it could not have been much.

During these last, interminable months, two fond visions were never far away from her mind, those of the lamented Judge Lord and the lost little boy. The dead Gilbert, especially, found reference in her letters, and the most poignant mention of him by far occurs in a note she sent at about the time of her October 1884 collapse (the first anniversary of Gib's death) or perhaps shortly before. It comes in suddenly, at the letter's close, contained in one of her more affecting prose passages. Of itself, the quietly evocative imagery attests how powerful was the impetus behind it:

The little boy we laid away never fluctuates, and his dim society is companion still. But it is growing damp and I must go in. Memory's fog is rising.

4

Sword in the Family

A MONTH of mourning ended for Austin Dickinson on the evening of Thursday, November 8, 1883, when he paid a call on the Todds at their boardinghouse, where he was warmly welcomed. "I was so glad to see him here again," Mabel noted in her diary. Two days later he again saw Mabel, this time in her husband's college office, where he took her the gift of a book for her twenty-seventh birthday. It was either on that occasion or on the previous Thursday that he made an intimate confession that she included in a long journal entry on the tenth. Her account of his words, if accurate, signals what was to become the final turning point of his life, showing as well that the move he made now was fully conscious and deliberate.

Rather gratuitously, Mabel comments that Gib was the only one in Austin's house who loved him or who gave him any pleasure. Then she goes on: "He says he should wish to die if it were not for me—I am the only gleam of light in [sic] his horizon—positively his sole comfort." A month after writing those words, with the apparent consent and approval of her husband, Mabel entered a full sexual liaison with the grieving Austin, an arrangement that was to last until his death. It is not beside the point to mention at this juncture two related facts: Professor Todd was an ambitious young instructor at the college, eager for privilege and pre-ferment, and Austin Dickinson was the college treasurer, with full control over teachers' salaries, assignments, and general academic standing. The influence of Austin's back-ground gave him power in the college well beyond his nominal office, made his voice in fact the decisive one.

So far as can be gleaned from the available records, the sexual part of the friendship between the two was rather carefully approached, even planned. Through the month of November and the first half of December, all three of the parties are seen growing increasingly friendly, meeting at the boardinghouse or taking walks together out of town. On her own, during that same period, Mabel went off for several long carriage rides with Austin, also for leisurely strolls of an afternoon or evening, so that she was in his company at least twenty times in little more than a month, with or without her husband being present. Two of these many meetings, if studied in the context recorded by Mabel, give a clear hint of the direction the friendship was taking.

On November 17, for instance, there was a curiously "accidental" meeting in the street between the strolling Todds and Austin, who also happened to be out for a walk, and a certain Miss Glezen. As Mabel noted, this foursome then went for "a long walk out East Street," and the diary finishes archly: "We came home in a different order from our going." Austin partnered Mabel, in other words, while her husband gave his arm to the otherwise unidentified Miss Glezen, and one obvious significance of the switch is the fact that Mabel thought it necessary to mention at all. Two weeks later—there were a half dozen meetings in the interim—Mabel came down with a cold. At home in bed, feeling lonely, she notes that Austin came in and "staid a long time with me." That day was a Friday, which highlights the fact that most of Austin's walks and rides and meetings with the Todds took place on weekdays during working hours, when even a normally busy lawyer would have been at his desk. He and Mabel also met on several occasions in the Mansion, where Vinnie—noting with approval that her brother visibly brightened in Mabel's presence—was glad to see them. Emily, who must have known that the two were below in the parlor or the library, still failed to put in an appearance.

Somewhat surprisingly, it was also at the Mansion, on the evening of Thursday, December 13, that Mrs. Todd and Austin had their first full sexual encounter, involving intercourse, or so it is believed. In that connection, something that happened at the Todd house three days before deserves mention. Mabel's diary for December 10 states in cryptic fashion that "David & I talked until half past two in the morning," which naturally links itself with the mutual decision to allow Austin a place in the family bed. Since both Dickinson sisters were in the house that Thursday, the inevitable question arises as to whether they connived at their brother's adultery. The only other writer to deal seriously with the matter says that the act definitely took place "in the dining room" of the Mansion. If that is so, then both Emily and Vinnie may be exonerated of complicity. If the sisters had had a hand in the affair, then surely one of the several unused upstairs bedrooms would have been preferable, for that particular purpose, to the inconvenience of a dining room—though how it was all managed without the sisters' help and knowledge must be left to the imagination. The truth seems to be that the Dickinson sisters, like everyone else at first, viewed Austin's interest in the sympathetic Mabel as therapeutic, providing necessary balm for his sorely wounded heart. For this, they were willing to ignore Mabel's married status, and in fact probably felt deeply grateful to her. David's own cool forbearance, perhaps, seemed the model to be followed.

Mabel's schedule for the Christmas 1883 holidays had her leaving Amherst on December 20 for her parents' home in Washington. On the day she left town an incident occurred which can be taken as marking the rekindling, if not of Sue's full-blown resentment and jealousy, then certainly of very strong suspicion.

In the three months since her son's death, Sue had seldom left her home, perhaps not at all. Her first time out was probably December 20, when, after the season's initial heavy snowfall, she gave in to Ned's urging and accompanied him for a morning sleigh ride. Austin, also invited to go along, said that he would be too busy at the office. Then, after his wife and son had pulled away from the stable of the Evergreens, he walked up the hill to the Todd boarding-house. Mabel, her packing done, was glad to join him for a short, farewell stroll through the snowy roads south of town. It was a little beyond noontime when a sleigh drew up even with them, and Austin looked over to meet his wife's accusing eyes. Greetings may or may not have been exchanged, and Sue's reaction can be judged only by what Austin told Mabel afterward, or rather by what he left unsaid—back home, Sue had nothing at all to say about the encounter. "All is tranquil," wrote Austin a few days later, showing how badly he had missed the true import of his wife's silence. "Perhaps a little more attention is paid to my comfort and wishes, and perhaps there is a little air of having discovered that it has all been of no use, that I have not really been brought under." Those brave words show only that Austin had failed also to grasp the significance of a further change that now took place in his wife's behavior. Except for an occasional carriage or sleigh ride—in the course of which she need not bother meeting or talking to anyone—she entirely ceased going out and stopped inviting guests to her home.

Once begun, the liaison between Austin and Mabel quickly gathered momentum, continuing without obstacle or letup through the summer of 1884. Austin, taking turns with the compliant David at making love to Mabel, was able to blind himself to the sordid aspects of it all. In the letters and notes he now wrote Mabel, he begins to sound as if they were taking part, the two of them alone, in some grand, inspiring love affair, rivaling the most famous loves of history (he mentions several including Abelard and Heloise). By late spring Mabel, evidently feeling some need to justify what had happened, made her first journal entry on the new situation. Interestingly, she is halfway through the passage before she thinks to put her actions on a more strongly personal basis than that of giving comfort to a grieving heart. The addition, however, fails to obscure the fact that it was Austin's extreme reaction to his son's death that created the reckless, abandoned mood in which his philandering began:

My well beloved friend, my staunch adherent, my devoted ally, Mr. Dickinson, is tenderer than ever to me. We see him in some way every day. He has expressly told me over and over again that I kept him alive through the dreadful period of Gilbert's sickness and death. He could not bear the atmosphere of his own house, & used to go to his sisters' & then he or Lavinia would send for me—& it was in those oases from the prevailing gloom in his life that he caught breath, & gathered the strength to go on. And not that merely, for his devotion to me is so intense & thorough, & so pervades his life—*is* the life itself, he says—that he recovered from the blow enough to wish to live *for me*—for the seeing & being with me, and the prospect of seeing constantly more of me.

Whatever the two saw as their precise motivation, both soon decided that their affair—always ignoring the presence of the supposedly equally loved David—was justified by its powerful, not to say overwhelming attraction, spiritual, they insisted, as well as physical. Nor was either of them much troubled by questions of right or wrong. "Conventionalism," wrote Austin, taking ground occupied by so many in his situation before and since, "is for those not strong enough to be laws for themselves, or to conform themselves to the great higher law where all the harmonies meet." With this liberal sentiment Mabel was in full agreement, and she said as much in another unguarded journal entry made at a time when the physical accommodation of two men had become a settled matter of her existence:

[Austin's] life has been in all home things a terrible failure, and a sweet home has always been his greatest desire. I would give my life for him any moment. To think of all that pent-up, tender spirit, longing for love & home & going lonesomely through fifty years, coming to me, in all the wealth of a sad and strong, but never embittered nature, so beautiful that it is real pathos—so patient that it is God-like. And it is mine! Lavished upon me. . . . And I am not so wicked or so weak as to even think of the conventional part of it. Because he was entrapped like a fly in a spider's web, years ago, when he was a mere boy, into a mismarriage, does that in God's sight keep him from me, whom he loves so wonderfully? Of course not. Men may think or say so. God does not. . . . And yet I will never make David unhappy. He has been wondrously generous and noble, & I appreciate, & will make his life just as happy as every possible sweetness & attention can make it. But I cannot be untrue to myself and shut the door on my real self for conventionality.

Tucked into that same entry is the first mention of a hope or wish she was to repeat through the years, that a kind fate would summarily remove Susan from the equation: "I should like to go along in a serene, everyday, domestic happiness . . . & with one turn of God's hand he could do it. Perhaps he will—perhaps it is nearer than we think." Susan, however, was destined to remain on the scene for another three decades, outliving her wayward husband by eighteen years.

All the easy talk about defying convention did not, of course, mean that either of the two was prepared to flout decorum, or challenge public esteem. Everything would be managed discreetly, veiled by what they intended should appear an ordinary if close friendship, again of the Bowles type. As Austin carefully explained it to Mabel, they would adhere to a precise "policy": the walks and the rides together would continue, he would freely visit her at home, they would exchange letters, and in general do all the things they had been doing right along, everything to be carried off with the most innocent air. It was a plan, he said, to be followed "daringly, defiantly, brilliantly, its very boldness protecting us from all common eyes." The unstated but effective and quite practical basis of this exercise in "boldness," as Mabel described it, was Austin's own high standing among his neighbors especially as a man of known integrity:

Some men, I suppose, could not come here five times without the whole village being alarmed if they knew it. But with him it is entirely different. He has always lived here—all his life—is honored & trusted & loved as no one ever was before, not even his illustrious father, & grandfather & great-grandfather, who have always held every office of trust and responsibility in town. . . . He has always been on perfectly free terms with all the ladies in town in whom he was the least interested, taking Miss Glezen and Mrs. Emerson & Mrs. Tuckerman & Mrs. Jenkins & quantities of others to drive at any and all times—and most delighted and proud were they to go. So that his taking me is no more than that in the eyes of the village.

Within six months of the start of this "double life," as Austin now began calling it, the two decided that conditions at the boardinghouse were not ideal, much too confining, and rather exposed. When a suitable rental property became available, just at the rear of the Evergreens, the Todds promptly took it, moving in at the end of June. Thereafter they were able to meet and move about much more freely and easily, without being observed and at their own convenience. The move itself, and the procuring of the necessary furniture for the large house, imposed sudden expenses well beyond the Todds' capacity, and indications are that the needed funds were supplied to them as a "loan" from Austin. This was the first but not the last of the trio's financial dealings.

With the three mingling happily at the new house, the summer of 1884 went by smoothly. One mistake, however, made by Mabel at the outset of their new arrangement caused a disturbance that for a time soured her relations with her own close family. More important, echoes of it may have penetrated the Mansion. Also, it laid bare what can be called Austin's least admirable side, showing him on his way to becoming a practiced liar.

Mary Wilder, Mabel's eighty-year-old grandmother, was one of the first guests in the Todds' rented house, invited up from Washington for a stay of several weeks. As it turned out, the old woman's eyes and ears proved a great deal sharper than Mabel probably expected, and when Mabel's mother, Molly Loomis, also came up for a visit, early in October, the grandmother was ready with a full report. Alarmed at what she heard, Mrs. Loomis immediately summoned her husband, and through the remainder of the month the two lovers had their hands full explaining matters to Mabel's agitated parents. Two letters of Austin, bearing on this brief but obviously unnerving interlude, survive. Both were written to Mabel, and for anyone aware of what was really going on, they do not make pleasant reading. Fully conscious of his guilt, Austin defends himself and Mabel in a strain of lofty principle, while at the same time rehearsing the lies they are to tell.

"We are not to be frightened," he says boldly. "We are not of that cheap stuff. We are not afraid of the truth. . . . Our life together is as white and unspotted as the fresh driven snow. This we know—whatever vulgar-minded people, who see nothing beyond the body, may think or suspect." He is not denying fleshly involvement, of course, only saying that for them, it doesn't count. But he quickly makes clear that this "truth"—of which they are not afraid—is to be kept strictly under cover. In order to avoid harassment, as he says in conclusion, it will be best to "conform" to the standards of these same vulgar-minded people. In setting these thoughts on paper for Mabel, his irritation leads him to talk of his wife and children as if they were strangers, lacking legitimate claim on him:

We will be more careful—we will, for the time, be more abstemious of each other. I do not believe we are watched— unless by my own household, who subsist upon my industry. Still we will not presume upon that—we will proceed with caution—we will not let a spy have anything for his pains—we will see each other less often for a while—as often as we can, of course, safely—we will carry ourselves ostensibly in individual channels. . . .

The main charges laid against Austin by the Loomises were three: 1) he called at the Todd home nearly every day, mostly in the evening or at night; 2) he did not enter at the front, as would a guest, but invariably slipped in at the back; 3) he often stayed at the house long after David had retired, with only Mabel to keep him company. In addition, the grandmother pointed out, Mabel had begun to neglect both her little daughter and her housekeeping duties, even though she had the help of a combined maid-cook. As Austin promptly instructed Mabel, all these accusations were to be set aside as gross exaggerations, a malignant twisting of the facts. Blandly he sketches for her the proper stance they are to take:

> There is nothing to the whole of it beyond the fact that we are earnestly interested in each other. I see you frequently because I like to, and you like to have me. . . . Wouldn't it be well for your father—if he talks with you—to understand that these are the facts, and that if he has heard differently, he has heard wrongly, and is suffering unnecessarily, and causing you great pain?
>
> Ought he not to have something pretty well attested before setting me down as a sneak, and an improper person, given to mischief and treachery?

Eventually Austin himself spoke directly with both parents, taking them separately for carriage rides on different days. His personal protests about his "innocent" friendship with their daughter mollified them to some extent, though it is obvious that the mother at least was never again wholly comfortable about her daughter's behavior. It is just as well that the Loomises never learned about the next step that Mabel took in her precarious double life. From notations in Austin's diary it can be said with certainty that about this time or shortly after, he and Mabel began to invite David into their bedroom to be an observer—"witness," Austin wrote—at their regular Sunday evening lovemaking.

The intimacy among the three was so well established by the fall of 1885 that they thought of making it a still more convenient and somewhat permanent arrangement. The Todds were to have their own house, it was decided, in which Austin would be granted full rights of access. The property on which the house was to stand—situated a block north of the Evergreens on the far side of the Dickinson meadow—Austin would contribute free. He also cosigned a building loan for the Todds at his own bank, and himself prepaid a dozen years of interest. Construction of the house, eventually to be called the Dell, was scheduled to start in spring 1886.

Undoubtedly it was the several distracting weeks with her parents in October that led Mabel early the next year to make a rather unusual request of Austin. Wishing to guard herself against possible future charges of home wrecking (a revealing enough fear in itself), she asked him to put on paper everything he had been telling her of his marital woes, particularly regarding Sue's personal deficiencies. To this Austin readily agreed, but then he never quite got around to doing it, and on being reminded some months later of his promise, he definitely backed off. He didn't want to take a chance, he explained, of doing something that "reflects upon any other! may offend or wound." He much preferred, he added, to forget the past and concentrate on "my meeting you, and for the first time feeling clear sunshine!" When Mabel next posed the request, he again flatly demurred, managing in the process to sound like a careful lawyer trying to lessen the impact of a loose statement he has let slip: "Why do you care to have me put on paper what, involuntarily, I have from time to time in ranging moods dropped from my lips? You know it all, believe it all, and it is all True." That subtle "ranging moods" is the operative phrase. It comes perilously close to admitting that what he may have said about his life with Susan must be taken as having been dictated by the emotions of the moment.

At least some of the things Mabel had in mind are available in her own handwritten list, apparently jotted down as a guide for Austin in his never-written confessional letter. A close look at that document—published some years ago, and ever since doing its silent destruction on Sue's good name—is instructive. Its five numbered points are written in pencil, in Mabel's hand, on a torn slip of paper:

1. Fly in spider's Web
2. Entire disappointment in all so-called married life
3. Destruction of various children (not intimated but expressed)
4. Carving knife thrown at you & other fits of diabolical temper
5. The spoiling of your life until you found me—that is, only coming to your own after years of mistake and endurance.

The biographer who first published this list offered the judicious comment that "there is little to corroborate these charges in Austin's letters and diary" (and then proceeded to offer several miscellaneous, and very questionable, items in support). A truer and more precise way of stating the fact is

that in *all* the records presently available, including those
Austin left behind, there is nothing to support these
charges, certainly nothing of an independent or unequivocal
nature. Analysis of the list, moreover, yields even less that is
concrete or convincing.

To start with, the second item and the fifth say essentially
the same thing, so the list may be immediately reduced to
four. But both of these, items two and five, may be set aside
as the usual exaggeration of the guilty parties in a triangle.
The small amount of evidence that does exist, either way,
gives quite an opposite portrait even while leaving room for
the ordinary strains of daily life in the home. Of the remaining items the thrown knife may well be true, as also the fits
of temper, and certainly both strike a disconcerting note. Yet
on reflection, there is another fact or say possibility about
such violent eruptions that becomes plain. Very likely both
may be referred not to the marriage in general but to more
recent arguments between Austin and Sue over his consum-
ing attachment to another woman. If so, they have, of
course, no pertinence at all for Mabel's case. The spider web
remark, echoing what Mabel wrote in the journal entry
given just above, seems at first blush to have some rele-
vance. Its real meaning, however, to anyone familiar with
Dickinson biography, is easily discerned beneath the over-
statement. From the very start of Austin's courtship of
Sue—even before that, in fact—the attractive, intelligent
girl was a favorite of the entire Dickinson clan, father,
mother, the two sisters—Emily in particular—and even
including Maggie Brien, the cook. None of these was backward about urging a marriage on the young man, and he
himself, it can be reliably stated, was as eager as anyone for
the tie. It was not until much later, probably coinciding with
the start of his friendship with Mabel, that he would have
begun to think his marriage had resulted from a sort of

The two Dickinson houses, the Evergreens (*left*) and the Mansion (*right background*). Made about 1880, this is the only photograph of Emily's house taken while she lived. Just visible at the second-floor front corner of the Mansion is the east window of her bedroom.

LEFT: Susan Dickinson in her mid twenties. The photograph, unpublished until 1988, was taken about the time of Sue's marriage to Austin Dickinson in 1856. RIGHT: Susan in her late sixties. She is in mourning for Austin, who died in August 1895.

Mabel Todd about the turn of the century, when she was
in her mid forties and had become the leading authority on
Emily and her poetry. She lived for another thirty years,
gaining some fame as a writer and lecturer on several
topics.

Austin Dickinson in the early 1890s, when he was deeply involved in his illicit affair with Mabel Todd, a situation that became known generally in Amherst.

David Todd, husband of Mabel, in the early 1890s. He was a teacher at Amherst College, where Austin Dickinson was treasurer with nearly unlimited authority over the faculty.

ABOVE: Emily Dickinson in 1847, at age seventeen. In later life she became slightly heavier—Judge Lord jokingly nicknamed her "Jumbo"—and she arranged her hair less severely.

Lavinia "Vinnie" Dickinson at about age thirty. The photograph dates to the time of the Civil War; no satisfactory later photographs are available. Some two years before this picture was made, Vinnie had suffered the love disappointment that pointed her toward spinsterhood.

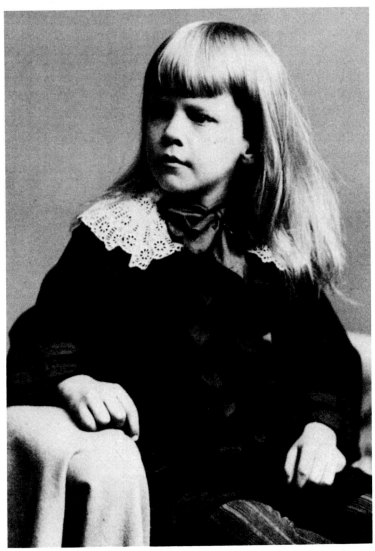

Gilbert "Gib" Dickinson, aged five. Some three years later, in October 1883, he died of typhoid fever, a sudden, tragic event that had disastrous repercussions in both families.

Martha "Mattie" Dickinson, aged fifteen, in a photograph made in the fall of 1882. For Emily's comment on this picture, see p. 17.

Edward "Ned" Dickinson, about 1890. An epileptic, he was to die in 1898 at age thirty-seven of heart failure having turned against both his father and Mabel Todd.

An Amherst picnic group of July 1882. At center, rear, stands
Mabel Todd. Seated at her left is Sue Dickinson, holding her son
Gib. At the fireplace is Martha; her brother Ned reclines with
tennis racket. David Todd, in straw hat, is at right.

Mabel Todd with her husband, David, in the parlor of their Amherst home. The photograph was made in 1907, when Susan Dickinson, aged seventy-eight, was still living at the Evergreens, a half mile distant.

family conspiracy (if indeed Austin himself ever used the spider web phrase).

The reference to abortions may or may not be strictly factual, though Mabel's submitting the list to Austin's inspection (or intending to—caution is required here) argues some basis in reality. But if so, then this much can be said: they must have taken place very early in the pregnancy and were probably done at Austin's urging, perhaps even insistence. He is reliably credited, early in his marriage and before the birth of his first child, with insisting that if he had three children, as did a friend of his, "it would cause him to start for Europe immediately & stay as long as he could." Told that he lacked the feelings of a true father, he responded that he "considered himself fortunate in being so." These are flippant comments preserved in a contemporary letter, perhaps spoken in jest, yet they cannot in conscience be omitted from the record. That he ever bothered recalling for Mabel these early views of his on the question of children may be doubted.

The liaison between the two, its true nature always carefully concealed, continued untroubled during 1885–1886. In that same period, on the other hand, Susan's role became increasingly a matter of helpless resignation. That she knew by now, or strongly suspected, that the affair involved a good deal more than companionship may be taken for granted, even if no surviving document confirms it. There is only a letter written in the spring of 1885 by Ned to his sister, then away at college, and it stays tantalizingly on the edge of real revelation about life at the Evergreens. The opening sentence refers to the difficulties of caring for Ned as an epileptic:

Mother has read me her note to you, and the amusement part has cut me to the quick—for her, who has given her whole life to me, to feel that she ought to entertain me is too much. As if I wanted anything else than to be near her—and try in my humble way to make her life a little less hard and solitary than it is. That woman is a daily wonder to me—and example—my only prayer is that Almighty God may leave her with us for many years to come—that *we* in *some way* recompense her for what she has endured here for us. If there is any beautiful, peaceful, restful place hereafter, and she don't have a seat among the saints and martyrs, I don't care to go there. Such superhuman efforts to keep up and cheerful for those around her, mortal eye never witnessed. . . . I would willingly lay down my life for her if for one day I could see [her] happy—treated as well as the servants.

In that letter, knowing his sister needs no reminding, Ned avoids mentioning the cause of his mother's unhappiness. But in one of his later letters, to his aunt Vinnie, he refers quite openly to Mabel's role in the tragedy that descended on his house. No longer the immature swain bowled over by Mrs. Todd's womanly charms, he bluntly identifies her as "a woman who has brought nothing but a sword into the family."

*   *   *

THE REGULAR SATURDAY rehearsal of the First Presbyterian choir was held on the evening of April 18, 1886. Practice concluded at eight-thirty, and Mabel on her way home walked across Main Street and stopped for a visit at the Mansion, marking perhaps the two hundredth time she had been a guest in the redbrick house over a period of three years. She stayed until ten talking with Vinnie, but, as on each of those other numerous occasions, there was no sight of, or contact with, Emily (then enjoying a period of re-newed strength, the doctor allowing her, as she said, to "roam in my Room" a little). Aside from the family and the servants, no one else had ever passed through the doors of the Mansion so freely or so often, and the question inevitably arises as to why Emily on all those occasions continued to refuse Mabel a meeting or even the slightest acknowledgment in person. Despite all that can be said about the natural restrictions of Emily's self-imposed withdrawal, her dogged unwillingness to face Mrs. Todd must have come to seem more than strange, even to members of her own family. To the question of why she so persisted, only one answer is really adequate, and it is tied to the larger situation involving Susan and Austin. It begins with another question: how much did Emily know, especially as time went on, of her brother's illicit relations with Mabel? The answer to that properly starts with Vinnie, for what she knew, Emily knew.

Undoubtedly the younger sister did take a hand, when asked, in aiding her brother's initial meetings with Mabel. She allowed the use of her private post office box for the exchange of letters, permitted them to see each other at the Mansion, and at various times took the trouble to write sympathetically to Mrs. Todd. However, she did all this, it is clear, in total ignorance that there was, or could be, an immoral side to the friendship. For Vinnie, this adored brother was simply acting out his declared right to have such friends as he chose, men or women. More important, Mabel's sensitive heart, her power of healing, had brought him safely through the dreadful sorrow of his son's death and this source of consolation no one wished to have end. Vinnie was simply the first, and the nearest, victim of the pair's clever policy of "boldness," concealment through the very appearance of having nothing to hide. The key, of course, was the constant presence of Mabel's own husband. In the eyes of all concerned, it was past belief that Professor Todd would have shielded a faithless wife, much less connived at her adultery. A few years later, when Mabel and Austin had become the subject of general rumor and suspicion in town—enough to disturb the church elders, it seems, who began to talk of excommunication for Austin—it was again the factor of David's calm presence that prevented a full-blown scandal: in the Amherst of that day, a ménage à trois was not even thought of as a possibility. Also subtly conditioning the aging Vinnie's attitude, by then, was her earnest wish to retain the sprightly, amusing Todds as her personal friends.

As with Vinnie, so Emily, yet with a significant difference. For Emily, Sue's trust and love meant far too much to risk their loss or impairment, even for the sake of a beloved brother. She could hardly forbid Austin the freedom of the Mansion, nor could she presume to restrict his friendships, in or out of the Mansion. What she could do to demonstrate her sympathy with Susan was to hold herself aloof. No matter how many times Mabel entered the house, no matter how much of a favorite, how much like family she became, if Emily kept her distance, then Sue would understand. Of course, this would not have been an easy stance to uphold: refusing to meet with an occasional guest is one thing, but it is quite another to withhold recognition from someone who in the space of three years calls at the house once or twice a week steadily, and spends some five hundred hours entertaining or being entertained in the rooms below. Mabel might well have wondered about such selective ostracism, though nowhere in her diaries and journals does she venture to question it. Perhaps she was wise enough to guess the truth on her own.

Only once did Emily try to reach out to Mabel, and that sole and tentative gesture may have resulted in exactly the strain between her and Susan she had feared. In the summer of 1885 Mabel went traveling in Europe with some Boston friends. While she was gone Emily wrote her a letter, the only real letter she ever sent Mabel, and Sue may have somehow discovered the fact. Actually the letter could not have been more impersonal. It was couched in broad generalities, was pointedly addressed to "Brother and Sister's Friend" (Vinnie, not Sue), and was signed "America." Even if the letter was sent, as it probably was, to satisfy a request of Austin's (it accompanied a letter of his to Mabel), Sue could easily have seen it as a betrayal.

At one point, indeed, Austin contemplated an action with regard to Emily which, had he carried it through, would have given her more intimate knowledge of the affair than anyone save the participants. When Mabel was about to start on her 1885 European trip, she wrote Austin an emotional farewell note. While she was away, the lonely Austin began paying daily visits to his sisters, talking more and more openly about Mabel. Soon, without apparent prompting, he thought of showing the farewell note to Emily, "that she might know of what stuff you are," as he wrote Mabel. A glance through the note is sufficient to show that anyone who read it could have little if any doubt of the writer's physical involvement with the recipient: "I love you, and I love you . . . my beloved, & my own, and my God-given mate . . . darling, my soul is yours . . . a kiss until I see you . . . you are woven in my every fibre. . . . Your love and my life are one and indivisible. . . . I give you my soul. . . . I kiss you, again & still again. . . ."

It is a curious question as to why Austin might have wanted his sister to see such a confessional document, why it was that he wished to prove "of what stuff" Mabel was made. A likely answer concerns a possible negative opinion of Mabel, or the affair, previously expressed by Emily, Austin hoping to counteract it. In any case, no clue reveals whether he ever did show Emily the letter, though the

possibility is there. If she did read it, then Austin certainly
would have been constrained to make further admissions
about himself and Mabel. How would the shock of even a
portion of the truth concerning her brother have fallen on
the physically weak Emily, already despondent over the
deaths of Judge Lord and her nephew? But that question
more properly bears on the subject of the next chapter.

During the month that followed Mabel's April 10 visit to
the Mansion, she was, on the testimony of her diary, in the
house again on nine different occasions, including one long
evening she spent there Easter Sunday. If she was still hoping for a meeting with Emily, that cluster of visits repre-
sented her last chance, for about noon on Thursday, May 13,
Austin came to the Todd house bearing sad news. Emily
that morning, he said, had once again collapsed into a faint
and at that moment was back in bed unconscious. Later in
the day Mabel hurried to the Mansion to inquire and was
told by the anxious Vinnie that there had been "no change,"
that Emily had not even awakened. Next day Mabel
stopped by the Mansion three separate times, in the morning and afternoon, and each time was told that there still had
been no improvement.

That same evening Austin, "terribly oppressed," came to
the Todd house again. Emily was still unconscious, he explained, was "losing constantly," with the added affliction
of very labored breathing. Her coma had lasted more than
thirty hours, and all had begun to fear that she "would not
wake again this side."

5

Called Back?

WHILE THERE IS MUCH about Emily Dickinson that remains obscure even a full century after her death, on one thing it can be said that there is general agreement: in her personal life no less than in her poetry, she had style. The fact is not without importance, for most often it is this unfailing sense of how she carried herself, that wry-tender slant she had on people and things, that is invoked to explain all those odd and endearing little touches that marked her last days: knowing that her end was near, she chose to make her exit as she had lived, with a flourish. Certainly she was capable, even in the looming face of death, of concocting all sorts of symbolic whimsy, yet there exists another possibility, long hovering in the background, that must finally be raised. As soon as the dwindling weeks and hours of her last days are examined under a sharper focus, it begins to appear that Emily may have deliberately hastened her own end. Radical as the suggestion will seem, especially relying as it does on circumstance, it can still be said with perfect candor that the only surprising thing about it is that it wasn't put forward long ago.

It was in April 1886 that Emily's disease went into sudden

remission, as Bright's disease will do, and she enjoyed an unlooked-for return of strength. The remission was brief, as it turned out, but it was in this interval that she managed to write and send what is believed to be her last letter, the famous short note to the Norcross sisters, her two spinster cousins in Cambridge. It read simply, "Little Cousins, Called Back, Emily." That terse and tantalizing phrase, *Called Back*, was long ago identified as the title of one of the day's best sellers, a ghostly suspense story that Emily and her cousins had read and avidly discussed. While there survives no direct or definite explanation for her cryptic use of the title, it is now widely accepted that she employed the words to voice some sort of keen premonition or foreboding. The incorrigible poet, it is assumed, chose this typically playful way of bidding her loved relatives a last good-bye. In truth, no other application of the phrase readily suggests itself.

It was also about this time, spring 1886, that Emily indulged herself in yet another bit of whimsy, if a touch macabre. To the puzzlement of both her family and her physician, she airily refused further medical attention, going so far as to decline even the meager comfort of her doctor's presence. On his last few calls to the Dickinson house, the nonplussed physician was directed to a seat in the main parlor facing the doorway. From that vantage point he was expected to conduct his examination as the sick woman, gliding along the hallway outside, came momentarily into view. "She would walk by the open door of a room in which I was seated," Dr. O. F. Bigelow recalled. "Now what besides mumps could be diagnosed that way!"

The abrupt termination of all such mournful doings was signaled on the morning of Thursday, May 13, 1886. Alone in her room after breakfast with the family, she fainted again, and was found some time later in a "stark, unconscious state," as Austin described it. She was put to bed, and Dr. Bigelow was hastily summoned from his nearby office. Rushing down Main Street to the Mansion, he reached Emily's bedside quickly and did the little he could, applying a mixture of chloroform and olive oil to lessen the violence of the convulsions that had developed.

That day Emily neither spoke nor recovered consciousness, and by next morning the hovering family members were forced to recognize that the situation was very grave. Adding to their anguish was the fact that Emily's journey to the other side was not to be peaceful or serene, for in addition to the repeated convulsions she was experiencing great distress in breathing. After some sixty continuous hours in a coma, late on the afternoon of Saturday, May 15, she died.

Judged by all that is known of her symptoms, the specific form taken by Emily's disease may be identified as chronic interstitial nephritis. In that case the immediate cause of her death would have been uremic poisoning—the kidney loses its ability to eliminate wastes, allowing noxious matter to accumulate in the blood. That is the orthodox explanation, obvious enough in the circumstances, and to date it has not been questioned.

Funeral arrangements had been made by Emily herself, hardly a surprise, leaving precise directives to be carried out by the faithful Vinnie. The body was to be clothed for burial in one of Emily's own white dresses, with a sprig of violets and a single pink orchid pinned at the throat. The casket, also entirely white, was to repose in the unlit library, with all the window shades drawn. Viewing of the corpse, even by close friends and relatives, was prohibited, a wistful attempt to carry the long isolation out to the fitting final inch. Vinnie, however, defeated her sister's wish by allowing the privilege to at least two persons. One, T. W. Higginson, reported that the dead woman "looked 30, not a gray

hair or wrinkle, and perfect peace on the beautiful brow."
The other, a longtime neighbor and friend of Vinnie's, who
had never met or seen Emily, was overwhelmed by "the
wealth of auburn hair and a very spirituelle face."

Services were held at the Dickinson house on the afternoon of May 19, which turned out an unusually bright,
warm day. Over the closed coffin a short poem, particularly
chosen by Emily, was read aloud. It was a spiritually exuberant lyric written by Emily Brontë (whose own approaching death had been marked by some curious events,
including a refusal to accept medical attention):

> *No coward soul is mine,*
> *No trembler in the world's storm-troubled sphere:*
> *I see Heaven's glories shine,*
> *And faith shines equal, arming me from fear. . . .*

A favorite New Testament passage of Emily's was read by
the Reverend George Dickerman of the First Congregational Church of Amherst, his eloquent tone framing the
words from I Corinthians, "O death, where is thy sting? O
grave, where is thy victory?" Proceedings closed with a
short blessing offered by Austin's friend Reverend Jenkins of
Pittsfield. Among the large crowd of mourners that overflowed the two parlors and the library were Mabel and her
husband, and in her brief diary entry that night Mabel made
a point of the "simple" services.

Lining up in the wide central corridor, the mourners
prepared to follow the coffin from house to cemetery, a
distance of a half mile or so, the whole route to be negoti-
ated on foot. Exiting the Mansion by the back door, the
solemn procession crossed the open yard, then passed
straight through the big family barn at the rear of the
property, and wound across grassy fields gay with flowers.

Slowly the long line filed into broad Triangle Street and turned north for the cemetery gate. It was a curiously public display to have been designed by the recluse, and for all her watching Amherst neighbors it soon took its place as one of the crowning touches of Emily's legend. Gleaming in the bright morning sun, the small white casket was borne along the whole route high on a wooden bier, lavishly hung with flowers, that had been hurriedly made by the funeral director. Supporting the bier were the sturdy shoulders of six bearers, all of them local laboring men who had at one time or another worked on the Dickinson house and grounds.

Emily's death, it can hardly be doubted, came to her as a welcome release, one for which she had yearned. But it was not so much escape from her burdensome physical trials that she asked. Her most fervent desire, as many of her last verses proclaim, was for a spiritual reunion with the dead Judge Lord. After his passing, vivid images of death and the afterlife became especially frequent in her letters and verses, all of them expressing an outright distaste for further worldly existence—in fact, it might be said that in the voice is a note of stark impatience, a wish to be gone. "The cordial grave," as she called it in one quatrain, was never very far from her thoughts, or the way in which continued earthly life now "deprived" her of what she wanted most:

> *So give me back to death,*
> *The death I never feared*
> *Except that it deprived of thee;*
> *And now by life deprived*
> *In my own grave I breathe. . . .*

Of the thirty or so brief verses that Emily wrote around the time of Lord's death and afterward, many go well beyond the exercise of some vague literary contemplation of

death, or a merely cerebral longing to be rid of fleshly
hindrances. As with the above lines, quite a number can be
read as very personal meditations on suicide. When she asks
plaintively,

> . . . *to that aetherial throng*
> *Has not each one of us the right*
> *To stealthily belong?*

her meaning even in so short a passage could hardly be more
definite. The word *stealthily* in that context will admit of no
other interpretation than self-destruction. Another half
dozen passages, all carrying an equally intense air of morbid
longing, are every bit as unguarded. Her cool observation,
for example, that

> *The spirit looks upon the dust*
> *That fastened it so long*
> *With indignation*. . . .

certainly expresses a feeling that bodes little good for the
writer's own dust. Several short verses specifically com-
memorate the death of Judge Lord, and three of them are
relevant here. In the first she complains loudly that she has
been "denied the privilege" of the tomb, a privilege already
granted her friend, and in the second depicts herself as a
frantic robin seeking her "lost" by flying toward "*rumored
springs*" (her italics). In the third she cleverly invokes grav-
ity to enforce a portrait of the increasing strength of the tie
between herself and the departed judge:

> *Each that we lose takes part of us;*
> *A crescent still abides,*
> *Which like the moon, some turbid night,*
> *Is summoned by the tides.*

Curiously, whether by error or design, she has reversed the true process. But in any case the pertinent fact remains unclouded: her crescent (incomplete) moon is being "summoned" by Lord's tide. That it is done on a "turbid" night perhaps adds to the inevitable atmosphere of morbidity.

The mystery of death, she admits specifically in another verse, to her "beckons spaciously." In still another she asks candidly if there isn't some more peremptory method by which she can avoid those many woes "the Future" always seems to bring, a question to which, as she knows, death is the only answer, death searched for and accepted:

> *Is there no wandering route of grace*
> *That leads away from thee—*
> *No circuit sage of all the course*
> *Descried by cunning men*
> *To balk thee of thy sacred Prey—*
> *Advancing to thy Den—*

Hardly to be denied is the ominously morbid cast of Emily's mental outlook in these last months of her life, so it should come as no very great surprise to find that, at this same time, she has fallen under the sickly spell of the two most famous suicides in literature, the overheated Romeo and the near-neurotic Heathcliff. Both these men, it might be recalled, took their own lives for the same reason, a burning wish to be reunited with a lost loved one.

Emily's preoccupation with Romeo's fate, until now unnoticed in Dickinson studies, is in no sense conjecture. The fact is clearly stated in a letter she sent an old friend in April 1886, a month or so before she died. Openly she writes that she has lately been much impressed by a passage from Shakespeare, and she quotes a line: "I do remember an apothecary." The words, from *Romeo and Juliet*, begin a scene in which the despondent Romeo, eager to follow the supposedly dead Juliet, visits an apothecary's shop to buy

> *A dram of poison, such soon-speeding gear*
> *As will disperse itself through all the veins*
> *That the life-weary taker may fall dead. . . .*

This whole episode, Emily confesses in her letter, she has been reading and rereading—in her own typically oblique phrasing she identifies the passage as "a loved paragraph which has lain on my pillow all winter." Very much off-hand, the remark seems to have slipped out almost unintended, but in that context "all winter" means three or four months.

Equally open and evident is the fascination felt by Emily for the dour Heathcliff, and here the influence proves to have been even more personal and potent. As is now well established, the novel *Wuthering Heights* was the one book above all others that Emily treasured in the weary hours of her invalidism. The reason was, transparently, her relationship with Otis Lord, a married man when she first fell in love with him (the case is even stronger, of course, if Lord can be identified as Emily's "Master"). Their longtime affair, innocent while Mrs. Lord lived, is exactly mirrored in the thwarted love of Heathcliff for the married Cathy.

It is Heathcliff's death, however, that is of concern here, and few readers of the Brontë novel will have forgotten that dramatic denouement. The darkly brooding Heathcliff, obsessed by the memory of his dead love, sinks into alternating moods of sullen apathy and wild exhilaration. For at least four days he takes no food and drink, finally shunning all offers of sympathy and companionship. On the morning of the fifth day he is found dead in his bed, his face lit by "a frightful, life-like gaze of exultation." The short period of fasting is obviously not meant to indicate that he died by starvation, and in fact, the purposely murky narrative at this point leaves a reader free to surmise other, more direct means, including the most probable in the context, self-administered poison.

But in any case, the story leaves no doubt of the savage Heathcliff's yearning to end his life, or his reasons for desiring it. More to the point—recalling Emily's own unusual funeral cortege, including the six bearers—before Heathcliff goes into seclusion for his last act, he makes some elaborate arrangements about his burial. Particularly, he takes great care to specify the exact means by which his corpse is to reach the cemetery. As the novel's narrator explains, "We buried him, to the scandal of the whole neighborhood, as he wished, Earnshaw and I, and the sexton, and six men to carry the coffin. . . ."

All these things may well be coincidence, even if of a fairly striking variety. Yet there remains an obstinate, nagging fact, that strange little note Emily sent her Cambridge cousins—"Called Back." Read in isolation, the words do have the feeling of a confession, expressing her sad belief that death cannot be far off. But when they are studied in the larger framework, the two words become much more portentous, carrying an air not so much of premonition as of calm, deliberate choice. And the more they are pondered, the stranger they appear.

In some special way, it may be conceded, the note announces that death is imminent. On receiving it, what would those Cambridge cousins, both decidedly the fluttery type, have been led to think? Aware that two or three days had already passed since the writing and posting of the note, they would have been forced to decide, or rather to hover, between two choices: either Emily was already dead, or she was still lingering on the brink. In reality, of course, there was a third possibility, for with the unpredictable Bright's disease, no one could have been truly certain that death was only a matter of hours or days.* Even as the Norcross sisters received the note, the patient might actually have safely passed the crisis.

Would the exquisitely sensitive Emily have sent such an alarming message as this if moved only by some vague guess or intuition? Better than anyone she would have realized that it could not fail to produce in her loving cousins a painful mixture of sorrow and suspense. The conclusion to be drawn seems unavoidable: when Emily penned those words she had good and sufficient reason, knowledge beyond the shadow of a doubt, that they would quickly prove true.

Of the three distinct physical symptoms that troubled Emily's final hours—coma, convulsions, and labored breathing—the first two are consistent with uremia, but the last not necessarily. On the other hand, there are several poisons which produce coma and convulsions, and which in addition constrict the breath. This is true of strychnine, for instance, which actually kills by asphyxiation. It was Austin who recorded the fact that Emily underwent great and continued difficulty with her respiration during that last, lengthy coma. In his diary for May 14 he wrote: "Emily is no better, has been in this heavy breathing and perfectly unconscious since middle of yesterday forenoon." The next evening, an hour or two after his sister's death, he adds, "The day was awful. She ceased to breathe that terrible breathing just before the whistles sounded for six." Taken together, these two diary entries clearly show that the "terrible breathing" began with Emily's initial collapse on the

---

* To put it another way, by the time a patient's condition was unmistakably moribund, it would certainly be too late for the writing of farewell notes.

morning of the thirteenth, and persisted, apparently with undiminished violence, to the moment of her death on the afternoon of the fifteenth.

In the very limited pharmacology of the late nineteenth century, strychnine was an important ingredient, and one prescription written for Emily in August 1885 calls for a half grain of strychnine sulfate. Also specified in the prescriptions written for her at the time, and for others in her household, are such powerful drugs as digitalis, belladonna, and morphine. Even if she could not have gotten hold of something lethal in her own home (in those days kitchen, washroom, and barn would have held all sorts of dangerous substances), or secretly by means of an outside messenger, she would not have been the first poor sufferer to hoard small amounts of her medicine until a fatal dose was on hand.

Many years before, in donning her famous white dresses and retreating within the walls of the redbrick house, Emily had quite deliberately put aside the things of this world. But her seclusion had not shielded her from still further disappointments as woman and artist, or spared her all the terrible anguish of the death and disintegration that overtook the beloved family next door. Disheartened and weary after so much suffering of body and mind, perhaps impatient of any longer courting a natural death in vain, did she at last determine like Heathcliff and Romeo to put aside the world itself?

6

Vinnie Takes a Hand

ONE OF THE very curious aspects of the life of Mabel Todd is the way her name became so quickly and inextricably linked in the public consciousness with that of the poet she had never met, seen, or talked with. Less than five years after Emily's death the first volume of her poetry appeared, edited by Mabel and T. W. Higginson. Within another five, Mabel on her own, or nearly so, had seen two more volumes of Emily's poetry through the press, along with a collection of the letters. By then she had also become, in lectures and interviews, and through her own writing, the public's principal source of knowledge concerning the poet's life and career. At her own death—it occurred in 1932, when she was seventy-six years old—her place in American literature as the prime mover, the indispensable factor, in bringing a leading poet to light was unchallenged.

In the Amherst of Emily's time, it was roundly and repeatedly stated, only Mabel in the entire town was fitted by temperament, training, and taste to be her editor. Acting out of "inspired devotion," as biographer Richard Sewall concludes, Mabel succeeded in convincing "reluctant men of letters and editors" that the strange little poems were "worth publishing." Barely qualifying the thought, Sewall further asserts that "without the spiritual kinship she felt with the poet and with the poems we might have had no poems (or letters) at all," and his final statement nicely sums up the feeling now prevalent: "Mabel Todd is rightly regarded as the savior of the poems." As recently as 1986, and in the face of greatly improved opportunities for study of original materials, another respected scholar is still able to proclaim that had it not been for Mabel's "devoted labor," Emily's poetry "probably would never have been published."

Some indulgence for those opinions, and others similar, it must be said, is warranted, for they were made in good faith and ultimately rest in large part on Mabel's own assertive claims. In a *Harper's* article of 1930, for example, she describes how a naive Vinnie came to her soon after Emily's death, "actually trembling with excitement," bearing the poems she had just discovered and urging that they be sent immediately "to some 'printer.'" Thereafter, Mabel explains, for "almost four years" she worked at Emily's manuscripts in virtual isolation, giving the demanding task "most of my time and all my attention." The published book, she concludes happily, "more than justified my years of toil with little encouragement except a sustaining belief in the greatness of Emily's poetry."

It is indisputable that Mabel Todd had an important role in bringing Emily's poems to publication. But what that role was, exactly, and whether it all happened in just the way presently understood, are questions never yet seriously probed. Surprising as that claim may sound, it is only necessary to cite a simple fact—by no means new to Dickinson studies, though largely ignored—to demonstrate its truth.

The book in which Emily's posthumous entrance into

literature was first lengthily portrayed, supposedly with solid documentation and of course with exhaustive coverage of Mabel's part, was the well-known *Ancestors' Brocades: The Literary Debut of Emily Dickinson.* That book, written by Mabel's daughter, Millicent, at first under Mabel's direction, was published forty-five years ago. While insisting on its "detachment and objectivity" in telling the truth about all the participants, it assures readers that it has held back no pertinent fact. Yet it makes not the least mention of one of the most important facts of all, one that colored and controlled much of what happened in both Dickinson houses—namely, that for a dozen years the married Mabel had been the mistress of Emily's brother. Conscientious to a fault, Millicent Todd was keenly aware of her own place in the story of a prominent American poet and of the need for absolute honesty in writing *Ancestors' Brocades.** In tiptoeing as she did around the intimate facts of her mother's adulterous union, she must have suffered much anguish of soul.

More surprising yet, *Ancestors' Brocades*, with all its evasions and concealments, remains today the fundamental text for those engaged in tracing the story of Emily's publishing career. It is also a large part of the reason why Mabel Todd continues to enjoy her special status in American literature. Without the indulgence shown to that flawed book, a fundamental truth would have been glimpsed long ago: Mrs. Todd was by no means in the vanguard of those who rescued Emily from oblivion. It was only *after* the success of Emily's first volume, with all the favorable attention it brought in literary circles, that she conceived her special devotion to the poet's life and work. Demonstration of that fact is surely long overdue.

---

* Rather in completing it after her mother's death. See below, p. 170.

★   ★   ★

THE TODDS' NEW HOME, a neat little Queen Anne cottage located a handy five-minute walk from the Evergreens, wasn't quite finished when Mabel and her husband took possession in January 1887. The noise and clutter of construction, however, did not prevent Austin from promptly assuming his special niche in the new establishment. At the same time, the compliant David broadened his own social contacts to include certain unnamed females of his acquaintance whom he brought openly to the house, apparently without objection from Mabel. Toward such women, according to her biographer, Mabel was always "willing to play friendly hostess." Of course, it was the hope of all those concerned in the life at the new place—soon christened the Dell—to keep secret from the town its true nature as a house of assignation. But this was expecting too much. Within a year the gossip had begun, initially hardly more than vague talk and innuendo, then steady but unprovable rumor, waxing and waning with circumstances or accidental sightings. During the next dozen years Austin and his two friends learned to live with this situation, always hedged in and protected by their policy of "boldness."

It was a month after the move to the Dell, and seven months after Emily's death, that Mabel gave the first sign that she was in any way involved with the dead woman's poetry. Her diary for February 13 records a visit to the Mansion during which Vinnie "read me a few more scraps of Emily's." Four days later she notes briefly that she has "copied a few of Emily's poems on the typewriter." But from then until June, if she was engaged in such work, the diary does not mention it, and in June she left Amherst to accompany her husband on an eclipse expedition to Japan, remaining away until October. Copying the poetry was not resumed until six weeks after the return from Japan, when her diary of November 30 notes she "copied two or three more of Emily's poems." After that, during the next seven months, Mabel spent parts of only six days working on Emily's verse, a total of perhaps ten hours sandwiched into her very busy personal schedule.

Much later, looking back from the vantage point of four years, and following the publication of Emily's first volume, Mabel wrote in her journal of the supposed wonderful effect the poems had had on her as she worked: "They seemed to open the door into a wider universe than the little sphere surrounding me which so often hurt and compressed me. . . . Most of them I came to know lovingly by heart, and I was strengthened and uplifted. I felt their genius." If that is true, then a very strange anomaly indeed appears in the records, for nowhere in her well-kept diaries for this entire period, nowhere in her voluminous journals, did she bother to set down a single word about the magic she felt in Emily's poems. Nor did she do so later, when at Vinnie's invitation she took a more direct hand in the copying (at only one point in her journals does she mention poetry, quoting whole a favorite sonnet, one of small pretensions written by the even then minor Lucy Larcom). In the four and a half years between May 1886 and mid-November 1890, when the first volume of poetry was issued, Mabel's journal contains nineteen separate entries, all couched in her ordinary confessional style. Throughout, there is no mention of, or reference to, the poems, none to Emily's genius, no explanation of how the poems had opened metaphysical doors for her, not a single remark on a particular verse or image or idea. Her daily diary during those same years, while briefly recording the various hours of copying, also fails to provide any evaluation of, or slightest reference to, any of the hundreds of verses passing under her eyes.

As is now well understood, the large batch of poems found by Vinnie in the week following Emily's death—some seven hundred manuscript poems locked away in a box, then hundreds more turned up in various places—had soon been sent next door and given into the care of Susan. Actually all the Dickinsons in both houses had been quite surprised at the large number of poems found, surprised as well at the care Emily had taken to preserve them. "The extent of her writing," Austin admitted, his bemusement evident, "was by no means imagined by any of them." Vinnie, exuberant at the discovery of so large a body of work, jubilant with what she several times called "a Joan of Arc feeling," assumed that Susan shared her desire to "magnify" her sister's name. With that hope, it can safely be said, Susan entirely agreed, for she was the one person in Amherst who truly understood Emily's unique personality and temperament and who realized, to a more than ordinary extent, what she had accomplished as a poet.

That assessment of Susan in relation to her sister-in-law is in no way gratuitous. Apart from the known facts of their long friendship, additional documentation is at hand in the sorrowing and tender obituary Susan wrote for Emily, which was published in the *Springfield Republican* on May 18, the day before the funeral. The date is pertinent, for it establishes that the essay—of fair length at eight hundred words—was composed very quickly, and of course under the intensest sort of emotional pressure. The actual time occupied in the writing could have been no more than a few hours, certainly less than a day (the manuscript must have reached Springfield and the offices of the *Republican* by the afternoon or evening of the seventeenth). What Susan says of Emily in this first (and for many still the best) evocation of her friend's distinctive spirit is clearly not the product of a moment's hurried thought but draws on long years of intimacy, as well as much concerned pondering. Excerpts from it have appeared from time to time but only by reading it whole can its special insights and pointed elegance be appreciated:

Miss Emily Dickinson of Amherst

The death of Miss Emily Dickinson, daughter of the late Edward Dickinson, at Amherst on Saturday, makes another sad inroad on the small circle so long occupying the old family mansion. It was for a long generation overlooked by death, and one passing in and out there thought of old-fashioned times, when parents and children grew up and passed maturity together, in lives of singular uneventfulness, unmarked by sad or joyous crises.

Very few in the village, except among the older inhabitants, knew Miss Emily personally, although the facts of her seclusion and her intellectual brilliancy were familiar Amherst traditions. There are many houses of all classes into which her treasures of fruit and flowers and ambrosial dishes for the sick and well were constantly sent, that will forever miss those evidences of her unselfish consideration, and mourn afresh that she screened herself from close acquaintance. As she passed on in life, her sensitive nature shrank from much personal contact with the world, and more and more turned to her own large wealth of individual resources for companionship, sitting thenceforth, as someone said of her, "in the light of her own fire."

Not disappointed with the world, not an invalid until within the past two years, not from any lack of sympathy, not because she was insufficient for any mental work or social career—her endowments being so exceptional—but the "mesh of her soul," as Browning calls the body, was too rare, and the sacred quiet of her own home proved the fit atmosphere for her worth and work.

All that must be inviolate. One can only speak of "duties beautifully done"; of her gentle tillage of the rare flowers filling her conservatory, into which, as into the heavenly

Paradise, entered nothing that could defile, and which was ever abloom in frost or sunshine, so well she knew her subtle chemistries; of her tenderness to all in the home circle; her gentlewoman's grace and courtesy to all who served in house and grounds; her quick and rich response to all who rejoiced or suffered at home, or among her wide circle of friends the world over. This side of her nature was to her the real entity in which she rested, so simple and strong was her instinct that a woman's hearthstone was her shrine.

Her talk and her writings were like no one's else, and although she never published a line, now and then some enthusiastic literary friend would turn love to larceny, and cause a few verses surreptitiously obtained to be printed. Thus, and through other natural ways, many saw and admired her verses, and in consequence frequently notable persons paid her visits, hoping to overcome the protest of her own nature and gain a promise of occasional contributions, at least, to various magazines. She withstood even the fascinations of Mrs. Helen Jackson, who earnestly sought her co-operation in a novel of the No Name series, although one little poem somehow strayed into the volume of verse which appeared in that series. Her pages would ill have fitted even so attractive a story as "Mercy Philbrick's Choice," unwilling though a large part of the literary public were to believe that she had no part in it. "Her wagon was hitched to a star,"—and who could ride or write with such a voyager?

A Damascus blade gleaming and glancing in the sun was her wit. Her swift poetic rapture was like the long glistening note of a bird one hears in the June woods at high noon, but can never see. Like a magician she caught the shadowy apparitions of her brain and tossed them in startling picturesqueness to her friends, who, charmed with their simplicity and homeliness as well as profundity, fretted that she had so easily made palpable the tantalizing fancies forever eluding their bungling, fettered grasp. So intimate and passionate was her love of Nature, she seemed herself a part of the high March sky, the summer day and bird-call. Keen and eclectic in her literary tastes, she sifted libraries to Shakespeare and Browning; quick as the electric spark in her intuitions and analyses, she seized the kernel instantly, almost impatient of the fewest words by which she must make her revelation.

To her life was rich, and all aglow with God and immortality. With no creed, no formulated faith, hardly knowing the names of dogmas, she walked this life with the gentleness and reverence of old saints, with the firm step of martyrs who sing while they suffer. How better note the flight of this "soul of fire in a shell of pearl" than by her own words?—

> *Morns like these, we parted;*
> *Noons like these, she rose;*
> *Fluttering first, then firmer,*
> *To her fair repose.*

No wonder T. W. Higginson wanted to adapt this obituary essay—he called it a "sketch"—as the preface in the first volume of Emily's poetry, a desire he expressed to Mabel by letter in August 1890. The fact that it was not done may be added to the list of those numerous small mysteries still unsolved in Dickinson studies.

In the light of the earnest and delicately knowing sentiments in the obituary, particularly in what is said about the poems, the circumstance that it was *not* Susan who shepherded the poems to publication is puzzling. Some attempt to explain what appears to be her failure in the matter, beyond those superficial reasons usually assigned (lack of faith, sheer unconcern, timidity, laziness, absorption in her own daughter's writing career), is needed if the narrative of Emily's debut is to be either complete or coherent.

Counting the many poems Emily had personally sent her, and the boxful that Vinnie turned over, by early summer of 1886 Susan had in her possession at least a thousand of Emily's verses. She also had some 250 of Emily's letters, those written to herself and Austin, and she had access to several hundred more she knew to be held by such as the Norcross sisters and the Bowles and Holland families. That she anticipated publishing not only the poems but many of the letters is clear from what she said later, but at first she understandably concentrated on the poems. It was just here, however, before she could get fairly started, that she encountered what seemed to her a nearly insurmountable obstacle: the disapproval expressed directly to her in person by T. W. Higginson.

In Dickinson biography it is well known that Higginson came down from Boston to attend Emily's funeral. But consistently overlooked is a return visit he made to Amherst four months later, on September 29, during which he stayed overnight at the Evergreens. The actual purpose of this second visit goes unexplained, but his presence in town at just that moment was to prove decisive for the poems. In the course of his afternoon and evening with the Dickinsons it is certain that he took part in some serious talk about the hoard of verse recently uncovered. It is also certain that in some way he informed his hosts that Emily's poems were— to quote what appears to have been his own term— "unpresentable." Their supposed defects, he meant, would prevent any publisher, even one able to appreciate the poems' undoubted excellencies, from accepting them as even marginally marketable. Whether he rendered this discouraging verdict after reading any of the just-found manuscripts cannot be said, and perhaps he was simply recalling his fixed reaction to the hundred or so poems Emily had sent him during a period of twenty-five years. Either way it was a fateful pronouncement. Four years later, after the poems had found a publisher—under Higginson's sponsorship!—Susan was not timid in reminding him of his former negative attitude and how she had been "held back" from publication because of it. "My own taste must be my own," she wrote him in forthright self-defense, "but a market judgment I have none of, and shrank from going contrary to your practical opinion in the matter. I think this much is due myself—my lifelong intimacy with Emily, my equally long, deep appreciation of her genius. . . . My own self respect and regard for yourself seemed to demand just this."

In addressing her disclaimer to Higginson it may seem that Susan protests too much, implying that, for her, there was no appeal from his verdict. A mature woman possessed of true mental sophistication, she must have understood that in literary matters such as these, opinions may differ, often radically, even among professionals. No doubt she was disheartened by Higginson's authoritative air, but probably an added reason may be found in the disturbed state of her personal life just then, her daily need to face the brooding shame of the little Queen Anne house. Nothing specific shows how Susan was coping with her husband's regular visits to the Dell, but there is one casual sentence in another of her letters written at this time which supplies a broad hint about the fright she had begun to feel. In the letter she admits to having moved slowly about Emily's poems, and she adds that she did so "dreading publicity for us all." The probing light of fame, she felt, even in a moderate amount, might uncover for all to see the family tragedy then starting to build to its climax. Instinctively she turned from anything that threatened to bring her disintegrating marriage to the ultimate disaster of public notice, so that in this initial phase, at least, it may be said that Emily's poems were in some sense a victim of her brother's infidelity.

During the fall of 1886, through the whole of 1887, and on into the spring of 1888—while Austin, Mabel, and

David became the targets of increasing town gossip—Susan did nothing with the poems except try the fate of a few with magazines, mostly without success. Then, at some unknown point, she decided they should not be submitted to the glare of formal publication at all. Instead, she would preserve them by means of private printing, and for this she envisioned a large and varied format including both poetry and letters, along with examples of Emily's humor and "quaint bits to my children." That way, as she said correctly enough, "I should have forestalled criticism"—and of course avoided publicity. That this was her final position after two years of pondering may be doubted, but in any event, by then it didn't much matter. The decision had been taken out of her hands.

During all the time that Sue had the poems, Vinnie had shown remarkable patience, only now and then attempting to hurry her sister-in-law (afterward she referred to "my disappointed endeavors" with Sue). Not the possessor of literary taste of any real force or refinement—though surely more than the bare minimum allowed her in Dickinson biography—Vinnie was nevertheless unwilling to listen to any advice other than that the poems, all of them without exception, should be made known to the world as fast as possible. Her primary desire, as she said, was that her beloved sister should be accorded the literary renown that was rightfully hers, and it seems unfair of Austin to imply otherwise, stating baldly that she did it without actual comprehension and "expecting to become famous herself thereby." In passing, it might be said that, left to Austin, the poems would probably have remained in manuscript much longer than they did, if they ever saw print, whether by a publisher or privately. Worthy of a closer look than it has yet received is Austin's very peculiar attitude of elaborate unconcern toward his sister's writing, especially in view of his own literary inclinations and his supposed rapport with Emily. The information readily at hand does seem to suggest that feelings of jealousy may have been operating, conscious or otherwise—but not every trail that beckons can be followed in these pages.

How long Vinnie might have waited for Sue to take action beyond the two years already passed is problematic. In any case, the event that finally galvanized her was outside influence, something unexpected in the form of still another Higginson descent on Amherst. According to his diary, what brought the busy Higginson to Amherst this time was a meeting of the "Philol. Com." (a great joiner, Higginson at the height of his activity belonged to some thirty associations, committees, societies, and clubs, including the American Philological Society). He arrived on the afternoon of July 10 and again spent the night at the Evergreens. Next day, after his committee meeting, he went with Mattie Dickinson for a leisurely carriage ride to North Hadley, then took the afternoon train for the return to Boston. Not covered in the customarily bare pages of his diary are such things as the people he saw in Amherst besides Mattie, and topics discussed. But it can be shown that he did see Vinnie and that the two talked quite seriously about the poems. Also, if words mean anything, it is a fact that his former negative feelings about Emily's verse had somehow softened, so that he now openly encouraged the delighted Vinnie to seek publication rather than settle for private printing. So much is established by a single casual sentence in a later letter of Vinnie's, written to Higginson in December 1890. Expressing her happiness over the first volume of her sister's poems, published the month before, she remarks in passing: "After my brief talk with you (2 years ago last summer) I resolved (if your life was spared & your interest continued), the poems *should* be published."

A last question tantalizes: how had Higginson's great transformation occurred? Had his own better judgment in some way struggled through? Had Vinnie in the full flush of her enthusiasm broken down his resistance? Did she accomplish the feat by peppering her visitor with a gentle barrage of the poems read aloud?—it is notorious how an appreciation of their deliberate technical skill is strengthened by a sustained reading. Tease the evidence as we may, turn it, pull at it, no final answer comes. Still, if that often undervalued arbiter, instinct, may be allowed a part, the palm goes to Vinnie.

★   ★   ★

FROM THE SECURITY of her parents' home in Washington, in April 1888, Mabel voiced her first open complaint about the turn her life in Amherst had taken as a result of all the gossip: "I feel as if I had awakened out of a nightmare, as I remember what I have been made to endure by people who are so far beneath me." Shortly after, she returned to town, where the talk, the slights, the furtive glances, and the "heartbreaking discourtesies" continued, though not to the point of making a difference in her behavior. With Sue, Ned, and Mattie gone to the Massachusetts shore for a month's vacation, the way was open for Mabel and Austin to indulge their liking for excursions into the countryside, so during August they enjoyed "unlimited drives," as Mabel noted, adding that "nearly everyday we went somewhere." Both, of course, were well aware that their goings and comings were duly observed by the attentive townsfolk.

Such conduct went beyond boldness to verge on the irresponsible, and by fall the pair were paying the price for their carelessness in the form of greatly accelerated rumor. On the afternoon of October 22, as Mabel was getting ready to go out, probably for a walk with Austin, David came home with some unexpected news that, it seems, shattered her. "Thunderbolt had fallen, and I was crushed," she noted in her diary. Whatever the thunderbolt was, precisely, she soon sent a report of it to Austin. In return he sent her his usual advice, weighted with his usual disdain, as well as an uncharacteristic effort at tongue-in-cheek humor: "Keep cool & own yourself. If you have done anything you are ashamed of, repent & begin anew, and better. If you have not, don't let gossip of weaklings upset you. Truth & right come out top at last. The world is too large and interesting, & is not to be given up because gnats and gadflies, and carrion birds find a place in it." His urging self-control on Mabel didn't help much this time, and a month later she came back at him with an outright demand that he do something about the situation, beginning with his own family. The belief she here expresses—that if Sue, Ned, and Mattie could be neutralized, her troubles in town would be over—is a measure of how far from the reality she had drifted:

I have been very loyal to you, so loyal that the bare thought of whether it is all worthwhile had never entered my mind. . . . It almost seems to me as if there is a faint little shadow between us today—for the first time in six years. I am perfectly aware that I have brought it upon us myself, and that it is a great pain. I do trust you—fully, firmly, even when your judgment seems to me over-cautious. . . .

I see it becoming daily more impossible for me to live in the little town which is yours. I see myself more and more alone, and I know that it is all merely the deliberately planned result of a hatred made and begun many years ago. I see power over all this lying idly in your hands, and you the only person able to cope with this terrible thing. . . . The day has come for you to use just a little of the strength which lies in you against the stronghold of all my hurts. . . .

When you say that I do not control myself, you cannot know the almost iron hold which I keep on myself all the time. . . . I have continually put down the suggestion in my own mind that much of this pain was unnecessarily given me by your reluctance to step in and relieve it in the one place which caused it all . . . how gladly shall I see you do what you can in this line!

If Austin made a direct reply to this sad mingling of guilt and despair, it has not survived, but there is one fragment in a letter of his to Mabel, of uncertain year, which fits the situation in the summer of 1888 so perfectly that it demands inclusion here. In view of the fact that Austin had now been a husband for thirty years, and was the father of two grown children, the fragment does not make pleasant reading:

I suffer for every wound you have received from my family, but for the time have seemed powerless to prevent them. What strength I have however will be pitted against any more of them. I will straighten the matter out before the summer is over or smash the machine—
I had rather be under the wreck than under what I am. There would be several other broken heads certainly, and I would take the chance of coming out on top.

It was in the midst of this renewed disturbance, probably no later than mid-August 1888, a month or less after Higginson's visit, that an anxious Vinnie, bearing the box of poems retrieved from Susan, came to Mabel with the urgent request that she take over the work of copying. Higginson in Boston was waiting to read the poems, she would have explained, and he had also agreed to help in the effort to find a publisher. The original manuscripts could not be risked in the mails, nor could Higginson be expected to spend his time guessing at the uncertainties of the original handwriting. Readable copies were needed for all the poems found in the box. They could be done either by hand or on the new Hammond typewriter Mabel had recently gotten for use in her own writing.

Later (just after the publication and resulting success of Emily's first volume), Mabel was to claim that when Vinnie first came to her with the box of poems, "she begged me to copy and edit them—put them all into shape. Then she was sure Col. Higginson would write a Preface, and someone would be willing to publish them." As can be found so often in Mabel's personal references, here is another of her half-truths, but one which is rather cleverly stated. It offers no outright lie, yet manages even in so short a compass a subtle wrenching of the facts. That Vinnie "begged" her simply means that initially the busy Mabel showed herself honestly reluctant—no thought yet of "inspired devotion"—to take on a task that promised to interfere with her own pursuits. Vinnie's persistence, in the form of a second or third request, constituted the begging, and Mabel's assignment was merely to make copies of the poems. In no way was she to "edit" them (though it was soon realized that a copyist would occasionally need to choose among word variants that Emily had not made final). The second sentence of the passage brings the name of Higginson into the equation, but it does so in a way that makes his function seem quite incidental. The deftest distortion of all occurs in that innocent little phrase *she was sure*, for it stands in place of the *fact* that Higginson had already given Vinnie full assurance of his cooperation.

In turning to her young friend as copyist—it needs to be said again—Vinnie certainly never thought to see the name of Mabel Todd sharing the title page of her sister's poems as coeditor with Higginson. As will be seen, the results of that unexpected development, where Vinnie's relations with Sue

were concerned, helped bring on the final disaster. Meantime, it will be enough at this point to cite an unpublished
memory of Mattie Dickinson, recalled from her attendance
at her aunt's deathbed in 1899. Repeatedly the dying Vinnie
demanded, "Get that woman's name off Emily's books!"

Another prominent aspect of Mabel's involvement with
Emily's poetry concerns her supposed arduous labor in preparing the copies. Much has been made of her fierce dedication in this clerkly task, and by no one more than herself:

> The outlook was appalling. Emily wrote the strangest hand
> ever seen, which I had to absolutely incorporate into my
> innermost consciousness before I could be certain of any-
> thing she wrote. . . . And of the first box submitted to me
> there were fully seven hundred poems!
>
> Well, I began, and it seemed as if it were, merely mechan-
> ically, interminable. I wrote and wrote and wrote. For nearly
> a year I translated them into typewritten mss.
>
> . . . Sometime in the summer of '89 I copied the last of the
> seven hundred. They made an immense pile and weighed
> pounds.

Emily's handwriting, of course, was not nearly so strange
as all that, and Mabel's overstressing its difficulties—note
her use of "absolutely" and "innermost"—is typical. The
seven hundred poems, it might also be recalled, were all
quite short, averaging about a dozen lines.

Elsewhere concerning her year of dedication, Mabel adds
several pertinent and homely details about Vinnie's anxious
if detached and apparently naive part in the proceedings:

> Frequently [Vinnie] came by night to our house and urged
> me to work faster, telling me that Emily's especial friends
> were dying so rapidly that she feared there would be no one
> left to welcome [the poems] even if they did see the light of

print. She begged me to work on them every possible moment, adding that if it were really tiring (which she could not imagine) she would give me a strengthening drink once in a while if I would only come for it. And indeed several times I did stop work long enough to run over to the old ancestral mansion across the meadow, to take a milk and egg and whiskey combination most delicious.

It is a peculiarity of Mabel's temperament that in her steady use of innuendo, half-truth, and what can only be termed double-talk, she is oblivious to the threat of exposure posed by her own carefully preserved records. Here, preeminently, is such an instance, for the story told by the diaries and journals for 1888 and 1889 wholly contradicts the claim of endless, dogged labor on the poems. Quite the opposite is true, for it is clear that Mabel gave her attention to the copying in very leisurely fashion. In the whole second half of 1888, for example, July to December, she worked at the poems on parts of only ten different days, perhaps forty hours in all, producing finished manuscript on about 200 poems. And with the new year of 1889 she turned for help to a local woman who in the space of several months made handwritten copies of another 180. The remaining 250 (the true total was somewhat less than 700) were finished off by Mabel in quite desultory fashion during the first eight months of the year, so that it was October 1889 before the poems were ready for Higginson's perusal. But it was not the difficulty of the task that had consumed the time. The delay arose solely from the fact that for Mrs. Todd—even if she failed to record a few copying days, which is likely—the poems were no more than a minor occupation.

Mabel's falsifications, made later in order to gain her a place among Emily's earliest believers, are doubly unfortunate in that they obscure the good work she *did* do. After all, despite the many distractions of her own busy life, she completed the task assigned her, even if belatedly, and she did get the poems into Higginson's hands. For that accomplishment, mechanical though it was, she deserves gratitude. Unhappily, the part she played in what happened next was another matter, for she could not refrain from introducing a final sly twist into the equation.

Originally the pile of copied poems was to have been sent to Higginson in Boston by post. But circumstances (a personal matter connected with Mabel's family) at the last moment called for Mabel herself to be there, so it was agreed that she herself would carry the poems to Higginson. This she did, and on November 6, at an arranged meeting in the home of one of her Boston relatives, she put the poems into his hands. Her diary entry for that day shows that the meeting went pretty much as expected, with some talk about the poems following a quick reading: "In the afternoon I went to Caro's and Col. Higginson came. He staid an hour or more, & we examined the poems and discussed the best way of editing them. Then I sang awhile and came back for dinner."★ Later, however, much later, Mabel was to recall something about that meeting which, unaccountably, had not found its way that evening into the diary—the curious circumstance that had it not been for her own quick action, a discouraged Higginson might have given the whole thing up:

Col. Higginson called upon me and looked [the poems] over with me. He did not think a volume advisable—they were too crude in form, he said, and the public would not accept even fine ideas in such rough and mystical dress—so hard to elucidate.

★ "Editing" here means selecting and arranging in sequence.

But I read him nearly a dozen of my favorites, and he was greatly astonished—said he had no idea there were so many in passably conventional form, and said if I would classify them all into A B and C he would look them over later in the winter. So I did that very carefully, and sent them to him.

Why Higginson should have gone back on the promise he gave Vinnie, during his stop in Amherst the year before, gets no mention. But then, in Mabel's records neither that earlier meeting, so crucial, nor Higginson's own agreement to help with the poems is noticed. One part of her later statement may be accepted as factual: Higginson's request that she simplify things for him by grading the pile of poems. With so much to be said against her, this implied compliment deserves recognition: it was the first meeting of the two, yet Higginson was so impressed that he didn't hesitate to place full faith in her literary judgment.

At her Boston apartment—she was sharing it for the winter with her mother and grandmother while her husband was away from home—Mabel proceeded as requested to sort through the poems. But again, it was not the lengthy and feverish exercise so often described (she "worked hard for twelve days classifying the poems," writes a recent commentator). As the diary plainly shows, the work of sifting was spread over no more than four different days, starting on November 6. It occupied perhaps fifteen hours, twenty at the outside, and was finished by November 17. Next day she packaged the result—a total of 634 poems, as she precisely recorded—and put them in the mail to Higginson. To judge by the total, it is clear that her decisions during those four days, comprising one afternoon and three evenings, were based largely on impulse and memory, rather than fresh, careful study.

When the package of poems was put into the post on the

eighteenth, Mabel's involvement with Emily's budding career should have ended. If it had, much of what occurred
later would have been avoided. Of course, her involvement
did not end, and once more its continuance was a result of
Higginson's desire to escape a burden: by now aware that he
had found an able assistant, he meant to make full use of her
talents. But just at this point there was an unforeseen delay
as Higginson came down with a bad case of the flu then
epidemic in Boston. It was the following spring before he
was able to complete his review of the poems, selecting
some two hundred as finalists. His first submission, apparently, was to his own publisher, Houghton Mifflin, and
probably he was not too surprised when the offering was
declined.

The next submission, to Roberts Brothers of Boston in
May 1890, brought from the firm's reader, poet Arlo Bates,
the predictable mixed reaction. While praising Emily's "remarkable talent," he decried her supposed technical crudity,
then ended with a recommendation to publish, giving his
approval to about half the two hundred poems submitted.
The venture would turn little or no profit, he thought, but
would yield a decided measure of prestige, a more tenuous
recompense but one dearly loved of all publishers. It was
Bates's further insistence that the supposed flaws in diction,
syntax, and prosody must be corrected that brought Mabel
back into the picture, for this was work to which Higginson
was by no means willing to give his own crowded days.
Shipping everything back to Mabel, he asked her to "re-
vise" where needed in the light of Bates's specific comments. This she did in the space of some ten days, imposing
a more conventional tone wherever Emily's unorthodoxy
was too glaring—the first instance of Mabel's actually
"editing" the poems—and it was her competent handling of
this aspect that convinced Higginson she deserved recogni-

tion as his coeditor. The conclusion was natural, so it is not surprising that the same thought occurred at the same time to Vinnie.

Faced with the alarming prospect that publication of her sister's poems, if Mabel's name were affixed, might drastically affect her relations with her sister-in-law, a frightened Vinnie hurriedly broached the subject directly to Higginson. In a letter to him of July 4, while discussing the poems, she abruptly made her feelings known: "I daresay you are aware our 'Co-worker' is to be 'sub rosa,' for reasons you may understand." She could not really have expected Higginson to understand, of course, and here the veiled phrase must be given its usual meaning: please do as I say, for if I *were* to explain matters, you *would* understand. This time, however, fate was on Mabel's side.

Unable to decipher Vinnie's handwriting (always atrocious), Higginson sent the note on to Mabel and asked if she could make it out. She did so, but what she may have reported to Higginson, exactly, and what he may have said to her in return, exactly, are items now lost beyond any hope of recovery. All that survives is the report supplied by Millicent Todd in *Ancestors' Brocades*, that her mother explained the matter to Higginson and that he came back with a prompt "Nothing is going to be done about so foolish a request. It does not amount to anything." That may or may not be the whole truth (what Higginson replied to Vinnie herself appears nowhere). But in any case, when the poems of Emily Dickinson were published, on November 12, 1890, the volume's title page duly coupled the names of the famous literary arbiter and his unknown young helper, with the unknown given pride of place: "Edited by two of her friends Mabel Loomis Todd and T. W. Higginson."

It was a Sunday morning just over two weeks later that Mabel sat down to her journal and proceeded to pen at great length her own special version of how it had all come to pass. By then the first public reaction was on hand and nearly all reviewers, despite much talk of "defects," more or less agreed with Louise Chandler Moulton's opinion, printed in the *Boston Sunday Herald*: "Scornful disregard of poetic technique could hardly go farther—and yet there is about the book a fascination, a power, a vision that entralls you, and draws you back to it again and again. Not to have published it would have been a serious loss to the world." Or, as the startled Higginson himself exuberantly admitted, "I feel as if we had climbed to a cloud, pulled it away, and revealed a new star behind it." It was in the light of this heady welcome given the new poet that Mabel in her journal declared her ardent championship, and proprietorship, of the new sensation, without the slightest heed paid to anyone else, including Vinnie:

> . . . the book is out, and the notices are beginning to pour in. Of course there is some notice taken of the lack of form, but all agree that it is a marvelous volume, full of genius, and a legacy to the world. And there are hundreds of poems still unpublished which I have here, equally as fine as those in the volume. . . . I mean also to collect her letters gradually, and arrange them for a prose volume. They are startlingly fine.
>
> So this, in a few words, is the general history of what has occupied me a good deal for the past two or three years. And it has been very satisfying work. I grudge no hour thus spent.

That fourteen-page journal entry made by Mabel on November 30, 1890, much quoted from since its appearance in *Ancestors' Brocades*, offers as true an example of autobiographical curiosity as may be found. Where it looks back over the events of the preceding three or so years, it is shot through with falsehood. Where it looks forward, it accurately predicts what is to come, for it was in the sustained and usually discriminating editorial effort Mabel willingly expended on Emily's second and third volumes (1891 and 1896), and the two-volume collection of the letters (1894), that she earned a legitimate if small niche in American literature.

But in giving Mabel her due for this later work, primary credit for that first crucial volume—and thus for the unveiling of Emily as a true poet, one of the few—must be allowed to rest where it solely belongs, with earnest, loyal, unliterary Vinnie Dickinson.

* * *

THE UNSAVORY REPUTATION of the Todd house in the Dell reached a peak of public suspicion from 1890 on, ironically coinciding with the first spurt of Emily's fame. Thereafter the relentless pressure of the rumors and the subtle slights steadily mounted until, late in 1892, Austin began thinking seriously about taking Mabel and running away from it all. He would head west to Nebraska, he decided, perhaps locating in Omaha, where he had friends and where he and Mabel could start life anew (what was to be done with David gets no mention). But this drastic upheaval never came to pass, and it may be that Austin simply changed his mind, though a not unlikely guess would also see Mabel's sure hand in the decision. From all the signs, she would not have been prepared to give up her cultivated New England surroundings for any sort of frontier existence.

Indeed, so somber and discouraging did the outlook become for the two during the early nineties that there arose talk—only on Austin's part, it may be—of double suicide. "Why can we not join hands now," Austin asks suddenly in a letter of spring 1890, "and walk on and on in that enchanting path we shall sometime reach, that never turns and has no end?" A month later, with Mabel away on a short trip, the subject is still on his mind as he describes in another letter how he wishes "that we had given ourselves to be whirled anywhere, even into eternity—so we were together." A week after that he is heard declaring directly and openly that "a man who would die for another, or with another, is not a coward, and you know I would do either for you—and find sweet pleasure in it." Another two days and he informs Mabel that he has been up to the town cemetery looking for "the sweetest, daintiest spot for two wild lovers to sometime lie together."

These morbid thoughts, it is plain, grew directly from the hopelessness and spiritual fatigue implicit in any such relationship. In that connection there is one further suggestion that may be offered—at least it should not be ignored—based on an incident preserved in, of all places, Martha Dickinson's memory. In her second book about Emily, published in 1932, she writes of a certain episode, year not given, in which Austin received one day in his law office an official visit from an elder of his church, the First Congregational. While the anecdote is told with a lighthearted air, it is decidedly peculiar even on its surface:

> . . . there was a tilt, however, between the church and its most prominent supporter. Austin, who suspected the object of the visiter who waited upon him at his law office—a good old deacon rather at a loss how to proceed with his errand, since the Squire was always on the Parish Committee and too valuable an asset to affront—went on writing till the caller coughed impressively. Throughout the discourse that followed—setting forth the delinquencies of his individual interpretation of belief—the writing went on; and at the finish the Squire's eyes were kindly and amused as he said heartily: "Excommunicate away, Deacon! That's all right.

Bear you no ill will. I'm making out an important paper for a man just now. I'll bid you good morning." Nothing ever came of it.

Perhaps her father's eyes were not so kindly and amused as Mattie liked to recall, perhaps she never did see how improbable it was to think of Austin being put out of the church he helped build on some vague question of doctrinal disagreement or "delinquency." Perhaps she really did miss the link between this strange, if fleeting incident and the increasingly public scandal of her father's double life.

As it happened, the two did not move away from Amherst, nor did they end their lives. They remained to become the focus of pervasive and continuing, if never quite certain, rumor, even as Mabel took the principal part in shepherding Emily's writings into print and complaining all the while of "small, narrow-minded people and their unchristian actions." At last it was Austin's weakened heart that brought both the talk and his life to a halt. After suffering through a month's bedridden illness in the summer of 1895, he died. And that fact, perhaps, explains why nothing ever came of the deacon's visit.

7

Lawsuit: The Final Puzzle

SHORTLY BEFORE SEVEN O'CLOCK on the evening of February 7, 1896, Vinnie Dickinson answered the front doorbell and found a smiling Mabel Todd standing on the doorstep. With her was a man whom Vinnie did not recognize until Mabel introduced him as Timothy Spaulding of Northampton. Then, shaking his hand, she said she had known his parents. The two entered the house and spent a pleasant hour talking over old times in Amherst and looking at the many antiques scattered through the downstairs rooms. When they left, Mabel carried in her hand a deed giving her ownership of an additional narrow strip of the Dickinson meadow, amounting to about half an acre, adjoining the plot on which the Dell house stood. The document bore Vinnie's signature and had been witnessed by Mr. Spaulding.

Walking back to the Todd house, Mabel gave instructions to her companion that the deed should not be registered. She wanted to delay its entry on the public record, she explained, a suggestion Vinnie had made to her on the way out, and with which she agreed. In reply to Spaulding's question about the unusual action she said that she and Sue Dickinson "were estranged," that between them there existed "a good deal of feeling." Her precise words, according to Spaulding, were: "If Mrs. Austin Dickinson discovered it was deeded to me, she would make trouble, there would be a row." Sue would also, she added, "make it uncomfortable" for Vinnie.

Following Mabel's wishes, Spaulding refrained from making the transaction official for seven weeks. The deed was finally entered on April 1, 1896, and a week later the fact was routinely printed in the trade journal *Banker and Tradesman*. Four days earlier Mabel had left Amherst for an extended six-month trip, joining her husband on another of his astronomical expeditions.

So much is fact. Everything else that transpired during that February evening at the Mansion was to be embroiled in dispute, eventually leading to the filing of a lawsuit, and then to a court trial.★ It was a stunning development, one which brought about the improbable sight of the sheltered Vinnie's being cross-examined on the witness stand. It also saw the Todds face a public accusation of practicing criminal deception on their friend and neighbor, a nasty if peculiarly fitting, even perhaps inevitable denouement for Mabel's involvement in the Dickinson saga. Today, sixty years after the renewal of interest in Dickinson biography, this rather astonishing episode still stands largely unexplored, not to mention unexplained. A closer look at the official trial record than has so far been attempted, however, turns up information that, despite its complications, points the way to some quite interesting conclusions. As might have been anticipated, it all seems to center once again on Emily's poems.

Involved in the lawsuit, if the interpretation given herein

★ Properly a judicial hearing, without a jury. But the word *trial* has become fixed in the literature, so it is used here also.

is correct, is a last-minute threat by Mabel to interfere with the continued publication of the poems, specifically the third volume, leading to a wily countermove by Vinnie. It very much appears, in fact, that in her later condemnation of Vinnie's action in the suit as lying and underhanded, Mabel was for once approaching the truth. Of course, she leaves out all mention of her own part, which also involved some characteristic last-minute deception.

★   ★   ★

THE MORNING SESSION of the Massachusetts Superior Court, spring 1898 sitting, opened to crowded benches on March 1 in the courthouse at Northampton, ten miles west of Amherst. At the plaintiff's table sat Vinnie, flanked by her lawyers, William Hammond and S. S. Taft, both of Amherst. In the spectators' section just behind her sat both Ned and Mattie, their presence making conspicuous their mother's absence. At the defendant's table sat the Todds with their lawyers, Woolcott Hamlin and J. B. O'Donnell, also both of Amherst.

Opening the case for Vinnie, Hammond stated to the court that Mabel and her husband had registered "a certain paper writing purporting to be a deed from the plaintiff to the defendant," which conveyed ownership of a parcel of land situated next to the Todd property in the Dell. Vinnie's signature to the paper, he declared, had been "obtained by the defendant, Mabel Loomis Todd, by misrepresentation and fraud." He then proceeded to lay out his client's version of the imposture:

Mabel Loomis Todd did previously to the seventh of February 1896, request that the plaintiff would promise and agree that no house should be built on the plaintiff's land next adjoining the land of the defendants, and the plaintiff assented orally and agreed that she would see to it that no house was placed on the land. . . . Mabel Loomis Todd did then further request that the plaintiff would give her some writing indicating the aforesaid agreement. And the said defendant, Mabel Loomis Todd did on the seventh day of February come to the plaintiff's house with Timothy G. Spaulding Esq., who was well known to the plaintiff, and whose family had been old friends of the plaintiff, and suggested that they come in for a [social] call and for that purpose only.*

During the visit, Hammond said, Mrs. Todd had "produced a paper and requested the plaintiff that she would sign that paper." Vinnie, thinking that the paper referred to her promise and innocently relying on "the good faith of the defendant . . . and not understanding that it was a deed . . . affixed her name thereto without reading the same." His client, Hammond made sure to repeat so that there could be no mistake, "did not understand at the time that it was a deed and conveyance of real estate." The Todds themselves had prepared the deed "secretly," he charged, without consulting a lawyer, and with "the intent to fraudulently secure the title to said land." Timothy Spaulding, who was a lawyer, had been used by the Todds not openly and in his professional capacity but as a dupe: Spaulding actually "did not know of the existence" of a deed until it was produced in the house by Mabel.

As his first and only witness, Hammond called the sixty-five-year-old Vinnie herself, and for nearly three hours she calmly and forthrightly responded to all his questions as well as those of the defense attorney. Her appearance on the

---

* That "call" here means "social call" is clear from other testimony, the difference becoming a critical point in the proceedings.

stand was by no means an *opéra bouffe* performance, as Millicent Todd styled it, and as she portrayed it so distortedly in the curious pages of *Ancestors' Brocades.*

Hammond began with Vinnie by leading her through the facts of her long residence and ancestry in Amherst, establishing her as a gentlewoman of the old school, necessarily naive in matters of business. Then he drew from her a recital of the so-called fraud's beginnings:

> Mrs. Todd asked me in August 1895, to give her that piece of land adjoining her own as a protection against possible future building. I should think that was the second week after my brother Austin's death. I do not think it was the first week. It was the first or second. When she made the request I was in the dining-room in my house. She asked me if I would give her that lot adjoining her own as protection against possible future building. I told her I would assure her that the land would never be disturbed, as it was filled with trees and shrubs that were very sacred to me, but I was not ready to make any land transfer. She then urged me from time to time, saying that I might die, to give her a promise, as I understood it, on paper, that there should be no building, in case I was out of the world, and finally I was persuaded to do it. I had not done it, but was persuaded I would do it, I promised her I would do it at some time.*

At the start of 1896 Vinnie's promise was still unfulfilled, and apparently nothing more had been said of it. The February visit to the Mansion, Vinnie explained, had come about not in relation to her promise about the land but because of her sister's growing literary fame:

* The printed testimony of the two-day trial most often runs together the witnesses' replies, omitting the attorneys' questions, except at crucial points. This was the ordinary practice in preparing trial records for appeal.

Early in the winter [Mrs. Todd] asked me if she could bring Mr. Spaulding to see me, as he was interested in my sister's poems and would like to talk with me. Of course I consented and they came. I knew of Mr. Spaulding. I knew his mother when I was a little girl, and she lived in town. His father I knew very slightly, but I knew of them. . . . It was evening, a winter evening. After personal conversation—it might have been twenty minutes or half an hour, a usual call, mostly about my sister Emily—I do not remember whether we talked about anything else in particular—Mrs. Todd asked if she might take Mr. Spaulding into the dining-room to show him my mother's blue china and some of the furniture.

At this juncture the record affords a detailed glimpse into Vinnie's version of what happened next, with a particular description of the crucial moment. The questions are put to her by Hammond:

Q. [Please tell us] whether your mother's blue china was where it could be seen in the dining room. Did you keep it there?

A. Yes, always.

Q. Please tell us whether or not you did go to the dining-room.

A. We went into the dining room. Mr. Spaulding was examining the china, and Mrs. Todd drew this little roll from under her arm and asked if now I would sign this little paper. Supposing it to be the promise that I had agreed to give, I signed it without looking at it at all. It was not open. It was simply handed to me where to sign, and I never thought anything about it. I have no recollection of Mr. Spaulding saying anything to me. . . .

Q. Who produced the paper?

A. Mrs. Todd.

Q. What expression did she use when she referred to it?

A. As near as I can remember, she said, "Will you now sign this little paper we have spoken of?"

Q. What was the paper of which you two had spoken?

A. Why, I suppose it was the paper she brought me to sign.

Q. But what was the paper that you had talked about before, really?

A. I supposed it was merely a description of the lay of the land, where it was bounded. I had never authorized its measurement. I did not know myself how much there was.

Q. Did you ever know Mr. Todd had surveyed it?

A. I never did.

Q. Did you ever know that she had gotten a blank deed from your brother Austin in his lifetime?

A. I did not.

Q. Or know that she had written out this deed beforehand?

A. I knew nothing about it.

Q. Had you ever known that she had employed Judge Bumpus about this?

A. No, sir.

Q. Or that brother Spaulding came there on purpose?

A. I did not.

Q. State all that you knew about the purport of Mr. Spaulding's call. What did you understand he came for?

A. I was told he came to see me. I was asked if he could come and see me on account of his interest in my sister; he would like to talk with me about her. It was quite customary for Mrs. Todd to have brought strangers to see me, because they were interested in the home. I supposed he was coming in that way.

Q. Had any other errand ever been mentioned to you by Mrs. Todd?

A. Never.

Q. Did she tell you on that evening that he came on purpose to take the acknowledgement of this deed?

A. She did not.

Q. Did you ever know of that fact previous to her departure from the country?

A. No, sir. I knew nothing about her sailing for Japan soon after, till my maid came in and told me what she had done. . . . I never conferred with Judge Bumpus or Mr. Spaulding about that deed, nor with any other person. I never saw it until today, save at the time I wrote my name. I had no knowledge of the fact that there was such a paper on the record until early in May, when my maid Margaret told me of the fact. . . .*

Hammond next tried to anticipate the two major rebuttal points he knew the defense would raise: a reason for Vinnie's having agreed to *give* Mabel the land in the first place, and a reason for all the secrecy about registration. On both points he drew Vinnie out with much skill:

I never had in mind an intention to deed this lot to Mrs. Todd. Until I was informed of a deed upon the record I did not know that she claimed to have any such deed. . . . We never had any talk substantially like this, that I would give her a deed and we would both keep it a secret from everybody for a long time. . . . She never offered me any money for it. She never talked with me about its being pay for copying my sister's poems. There was never any talk of that kind between me and Mrs. Todd.

Cross-examination of Vinnie was handled by lawyer O'Donnell, and he promptly tried to establish Mabel's work on Emily's poems as sufficient ground for Vinnie's giving

---

* The maid, Maggie Maher, had met someone at the post office who mentioned seeing the notice in the *Banker and Tradesman*.

her the land. In this, however, the prepared Vinnie conceded
little, dismissing the difficulties of the manuscripts, deliberately emphasizing Mabel's role as mere copyist, and concentrating on her voluntary involvement. "Mrs. Todd asked the
privilege of doing it," she insisted, thinking of the second
and third volumes, and pointedly adding, "I knew that she
thought it would be to her literary reputation to do it, and it
made her reputation."

Preparing the way for what he evidently thought would
be his strongest point in the Todds' defense, O'Donnell
asked Vinnie about Dwight Hills, a close neighbor of the
Dickinsons for twenty years. Immediately after Austin's
death Hills had agreed to watch over Vinnie's financial affairs, it being understood that she would make no move
without his counsel and advice. To Vinnie on the stand,
O'Donnell now stated that in fact on more than one occasion
she had lengthily discussed with Hills the *giving* of the strip
of land to the Todds, but had never said a word to him about
a promise to allow no building there. Vinnie certainly was
aware that Hills, who was ill and confined to bed, had
already supplied the defense with a deposition to that effect,
but the knowledge gave her no pause:

> I never stated to [Mr. Hills] that my brother had for a long
> time wanted me to do something for the Todds. I did not say
> that to Mr. Hills. . . . After Mrs. Todd asked me for the land,
> Mr. Hills being my financial adviser, I told him of her re-
> quest, and he said by no means to let any land go, that it was
> an inheritance of many generations back, and when I ceased
> to care for it, should belong to my niece and nephew. . . . I
> never used the word deed to Mr. Hills. I never said anything
> to Mr. Hills about the agreement between myself and Mrs.
> Todd as to having no buildings put there. I did not consider it

of any consequence. I did not consider it anything legal. It was simply a promise of friendship.

It was Hills himself, Vinnie explained, who "advised me to put [the case] into Mr. Hammond's hands." She also flatly denied ever speaking to Hills's housekeeper, Frances Seelye, at any time, anywhere, about giving land to the Todds.

O'Donnell then took Vinnie back over the details of the February visit, hoping to demonstrate that she had been fully aware of Mabel's purpose:

I opened the door myself when Mrs. Todd and Mr. Spaulding came. . . . We went into the library. We remained there, it might have been, half an hour. Mrs. Todd asked that he be taken into the dining-room to see some china that he was very fond of, so she said. While there she asked me if I would sign this paper, while he was looking at this blue china in the dining room. . . .

Q. Tell us whether or not the paper, the introduction of the paper had anything to do with your going into that room.
A. Nothing was said about it until after we went in there.
Q. And then how was the matter of the paper introduced?
A. Mrs. Todd, while Mr. Spaulding was looking at the blue china, drew out this little paper and said would I now sign this paper. I, supposing it was the promise I had made that no building should be put on that particular spot of ground, said I would sign it, and I did. I did not read it. I supposed it was simply a description of the lay of the land.
Q. Wasn't this the fact, that you went to look at the china after the paper had been signed?
A. No, sir.

Q. Now then, was it the further fact that when Mrs. Todd introduced this paper she said to you this was the deed or paper you were to sign?

A. I did not hear the word deed.

Q. Did she say, "This is the paper you were to sign"?

A. That is the way I understood it.

Q. Did she hand it to Mr. Spaulding?

A. She did not.

Q. Did Mr. Spaulding take that paper and look it over a little?

A. I did not see him. I do not remember his speaking. He did not say anything to me at all. . . . He did not point out the place against the seal where I should sign. Mrs. Todd pointed it out. Mrs. Todd handed me the paper and I signed it, and that is all I remember about it. . . . We went into the dining-room and stayed till this was finished and then they went away.

At the afternoon session the leadoff witness was an Amherst real estate expert, a friend of Austin's, who was asked to put a fair market value on the land in question. Far from the $2,000 claimed by Vinnie, he said it was worth, at most, $650.

Introducing the Todds' defense, lawyer Woolcott Hamlin minutely described Mabel's labors on the three volumes of Emily's poems, emphasizing the difficulties and her dedication. Then he linked the editorial work to the land as compensation, first through Austin, then through Austin with Vinnie, declaring that she had originally meant to complete the action begun by her dead brother:

Austin Dickinson, a brother of the plaintiff . . . was acquainted with the extent of the services which [the Todds] had performed for his sister, and had often expressed his dissatisfaction at his sister's failure to properly compensate the defendants . . . In the spring of 1895 he came to the house and asked the defendant, David P. Todd, to go with him and measure the said lot, having previously looked at the deed of the original lot. The property was examined, measured, and the said Dickinson jotted down the figures. He thereupon handed to the said Mabel Todd two or three blank deed forms which he had brought over and asked her to write upon one with pencil the measurement figures which he gave her. This she did, and he said that when next he should come to the house he should want her to copy it in ink on the other blank deed, and then he would execute it, but he died before having the opportunity so to do.

Called to the stand, Mabel proceeded to contradict nearly everything Vinnie had said, pressing home especially Vinnie's original agreement with her brother's wishes:

In early September, 1895, we spoke about the lot now in question. I think it was probably at her house. I think I told her that her brother wished this narrow strip of land to be added to our lot, and that he was about to ask her to sign the deed. . . . There were several conversations about that time in September and early October. . . . She replied to me that she wished he had finished the deed . . . but if I would sometime finish copying it in shape she would sign it and complete it herself. . . . On one occasion when I was at her house she asked me to go out to the side gate, she could see the meadow from there, and we went out. She said, "Now show me where the new line will be." I showed her as near as I could, slightly to the east of a certain telegraph pole. . . .

She said she would go and examine it some time in the night, but she would not go in the daytime. She did go one night, about nine o'clock in the evening, by moonlight, in early December. I happened to see her and my husband also saw her walking about this strip of land, back and forth, north, south, east and west. Then in a few minutes she came into our house and said she understood the boundaries of the strip, and she would be glad to complete the deed at any time I would finish copying it.

Not surprisingly, in Mabel's description of the February visit to the Mansion there was no room at all for Vinnie's version. But its added details, in spite of a lingering vagueness, gave it somewhat more a ring of truth than usual:

I asked Miss Dickinson . . . if she would like to have Mr. Spaulding take the acknowledgement of this deed, and she said she would be perfectly satisfied with him. . . . I saw him some time in late January and asked him if he would come some evening and he said he would. She asked me not to have him come by daylight. I asked him if he would come after six o'clock. . . .

He came to my house, and we crossed the intervening space to Miss Dickinson's house, rang the bell, and she came to the door. I said, "Miss Dickinson, this is Mr. Spaulding, of whom we have spoken." She said, "I am very glad to see him," and we walked into the library. I don't know how long the call was. We talked about early things, about her sister's poems, and the old people of Amherst. . . . I do not remember whether the deed was brought out in the library or later on, but it was brought out after possibly fifteen or twenty minutes. I said, "Miss Dickinson, this is the deed we have been talking about of that strip of land." That was in the dining-room, I think, because she got out her pen and ink, which was always kept in the dining-room. . . . In the conversation . . . it came out that she was perfectly willing to do it then, and she signed it, and she handed the pen to Mr. Spaulding, or he took it, and he put his name on the line next to hers.

Before the paper was signed I had it. I think I unfolded it and laid it out on the table. . . . Mr. Spaulding . . . turned it over, and said, "Miss Dickinson, this purports to be a deed of a strip of land next to the house that Mrs. Todd lives in, down in the meadow," and he read the dimensions, 54 feet one way and so many the other way. He used the word deed several times. . . . He asked her distinctly if she knew what it was, and she replied, "Perfectly, we have talked it over," or words to that effect.

At the end of the call, just as we were going out the front door, she said to me in a very low tone—whether Mr. Spaulding heard it or not I don't know, I haven't seen him since to ask him—"I don't want this deed registered, I want it kept quiet." . . . She said it near the door, in a very low tone, at the front door, as we were going out. We were standing together. She said it in a very low tone.

In cross-examining Mabel, Vinnie's attorney concentrated his attention on two things, the poems and the supposed deed, its preparation and signing. His questions, judging by the shortness and the disjointed tone of Mabel's replies, must have ranged widely, in abrupt fashion, and been posed in fairly rapid-fire style:

I never said anything to Miss Dickinson about a deed of this land until her brother Austin died. . . . I occasionally touched very lightly the claim that she ought to give me a deed for the work I had done on the poems. It is not my way to urge my claims. I think I mentioned it once. I had half a dozen, or eight or ten talks with her, possibly. I think the matter of compensation for my labors on the poems may have been mentioned once or twice during the autumn, October and possibly very early in November. I remember once. I don't know but there might have been a second time. I am not sure. She said she appreciated my work on the poems, if it hadn't been for me they would not have been published. To copy them was not all I did. It was not substantially all. We did not always use the first word. I don't think Mr. Higginson says so. He says we usually decided her first rendering was best. . . .

I did it because Miss Dickinson asked me to and because I enjoyed the work and thought there was real genius in the poems and that they ought to come out. I don't remember telling Miss Dickinson that I did it as a labor of love. It is possible I may have used that phrase. . . . When the poems first came out there was great interest. It has not been for some years. I have given readings from her poems, sometimes for compensation, sometimes not. . . .

I came to see Mr. Spaulding late in January. . . . I told him that I had made this deed, drawn this deed up myself, that Miss Dickinson had been out there and walked up and down the land and knew what it was. . . . I asked him to witness the deed. . . . I told him Miss Dickinson wanted him to come after dark . . . and he said "Why?" I said because she didn't like to have her affairs talked about in Amherst, she liked to do things quietly. . . .

Coming to the night of the February visit to the Mansion, Hammond very nearly caught Mabel in a slip. With one careless phrase she seemed to admit that the call at the Dickinson house had not been planned, as she claimed, and especially that Spaulding's presence had not been expected by Vinnie:

Q. The only object of your visit was to get the woman to sign that deed?
A. To get her to sign the deed was what we went for. That is what she knew we went for. That was the only object he came over for.
Q. He came from Northampton to Amherst at your request, without compensation, didn't he?
A. Mr. Spaulding never sent any bill for it. I should very

happily have paid him if he had sent a bill. Miss Lavinia knew what we came for. . . . I think Mr. Spaulding did not say anything about it until I spoke. I don't think Miss Lavinia said a word about it until I spoke. I had the deed in an envelope, and I said, "Miss Vinnie, here is the deed of that strip of land we have been talking about." I think I had the envelope in my hand. I had no pocket deep enough to carry it in. . . . I am quite sure I had it in an envelope to save soiling it. I must have, for I shouldn't want to soil it.

Q. What was the first thing you said?

A. I said, "Miss Vinnie, here is the deed we have been talking about of that strip of land." She said, "Very well."

Q. What else did you say?

A. That I think was in the dining room. She got out her pen and ink then. There was something said about her signing it.

Q. What was said?

A. I can't remember every word. She said something like, "Shall I sign it now?" I said, "Mr. Spaulding is here. Perhaps now is as well as any time."

Q. What did you say that for, if you knew that was what he was over there for—if you knew he came on purpose to sign the deed?

A. I knew I was going out of the country for six—

Q. What did you say that for? Why did you say that if you knew that was what he was over there for, and knew she knew he came on purpose to sign the deed?

A. I suppose because then was the most convenient time, because he was there. She wasn't like the ordinary run of people.

Q. You say he was there on purpose to see her sign the deed?

A. Yes, sir.

Q. She knew it?

A. She knew it.

Q. And knowing it perfectly well, she said, "Shall I sign it now?"

A. She said something like that. . . . I think it was a natural thing for me to say, "Here is that deed we have been talking about. Mr. Spaulding is here and you may as well sign it." Mr. Spaulding was courteous enough not to hurry her. If she wasn't ready he would come again. . . . I think I laid [the deed] on the table in front of Miss Lavinia. On the dining room table that is near the sideboard, that is covered with blue china. Mr. Spaulding was beside me. Just how we stood I don't remember. Miss Dickinson was next to the lamp; I think I was standing next to her, and Mr. Spaulding the other side of me. He was standing up; I think not looking at the china at that time. . . . Mr. Spaulding pointed out the place, but before she signed it, he picked it up and turned to the place and said it seemed to be a deed of the strip of land lying beside my homestead. . . . He used the word deed three or four times. I heard the word deed a great many times. . . . I suppose Mr. Spaulding put the seal there, I didn't. I didn't have any of those seals. I don't remember when I first saw the seal there. . . . He asked her if it was her free act, in some special words, I don't remember just how he put it. He said, "Do you sign of your own free will," or "Of your free act," or something of that kind, and she said, "I do." After she signed he took her pen and wrote his name. . . .

Hammond quickly followed up on Mabel's apparent slip by making another attempt to show her, even aside from the February visit, acting in a devious manner. Concerning the lengthy delay in registering the signed deed, he inquired, what circumstances finally led to its being put on record? In Mabel's reply a certain confused hesitation is quite noticeable:

I told him not to record it at once. I afterwards went over to
see him and he told me it ought to be recorded. I said it was
not her wish to have it recorded. I think I afterwards gave
him directions to have it recorded. . . . I did not tell him by
mail. I told him after a while to put it on record. I said, "After
a while." I left Amherst the 4th of April. I don't remember
that this was recorded the first. I don't remember writing to
Mr. Spaulding any such letter as that I was going to leave in a
day or two and to put that deed on record. I don't think I
wrote so. I may have written to him, but I don't recall it.

The defense, in an effort to enlarge on and confirm
Mabel's brief mention of Vinnie's nighttime excursion to
check the boundaries and layout of the strip, called David to
the stand. The precise questions put to him by the lawyers
on both sides brought out a fuller picture of what he and
Mabel had seen that night:

I saw her first on that land walking back and forth in several
different directions upon that strip, in the month of December, at night and by moonlight. She came after this, into our
house, that same evening. . . . She remarked that she had
been all over the strip of land, and that she understood about
it, what its boundaries, in a general way, were, and that she
was prepared to complete the deed anytime. . . .

Q. Where was she when you first saw her that night?
A. Within sixty feet of the steps of my house, ten feet of the
   southeast corner of my porch. I was in the southeast
   room on the first floor of my house, standing at the east
   window. . . . The sun had gone down but the moon was
   up . . . it had been dark for somewhere about four
   hours. . . . I was standing up at the window when I
   looked out and saw her. I do not recall anything special
   that called my attention to the window at just that moment. I quite often study the stars at home. Quite often
   from the east window. . . .

Q. How did you know what she was there for?
A. The matter had been frequently talked over.
Q. Had you ever said a word to her about it?
A. Not to Miss Dickinson.
Q. You can't say what was said between you and your wife, but you suspected that she was there to see the boundaries?
A. I understood that to be the purpose.
Q. Why didn't you go out and show them to her?
A. Because I had not been invited to do so. She preferred—
Q. Any other reason?
A. Not the slightest. I did not go out to show her what she was trying to find. . . . I watched her perhaps from three to five minutes. How long she had been there I do not know. . . . After I first saw her before she came into the house was, I should say, three to five minutes. I never had any further talk with her about this deed or about this land. . . .

For a fleeting moment as David ended his testimony, the specter of scandal seemed about to be let loose in the courtroom. Lawyer Taft for some reason suddenly switched his focus from the strip in dispute to the original large plot of land on which the Todd house stood. Taken by surprise, David at first stumbled as he tried to obscure the fact that the expensive plot had been a gift from Austin. He recovered only enough to make a weak effort at linking the gift with the work Mabel had done on the poems. But to make that credible, he had to tell a second lie, moving the start of Mabel's work on the poems back almost to the month of Emily's death:

I bought this building lot or got it of the Dickinsons, where my house stands. I paid nothing for it. I can't give the date when I got it within three months. I got it in 1896—I beg

pardon, 1886. I should say after Miss Emily died. I couldn't
say whether after the work had begun on these poems. It may
have been in May 1886, it may have been in July.

It is a pity that the lawyers' questions have been omitted
here, for their absence obscures the drama that arose as a
result of the two opening sentences quoted. The first answer consists of an outright lie quickly followed by an
equivocation, facts of which the lawyer was certainly aware.
His next question, whatever it was exactly, pinned David
down: "I paid nothing for it." That sensitive topic, however,
was not pursued by either side, and such careful avoidance
indicates a mutual desire, even a verbal agreement, to side-
step any and all direct mention of the Todds' friendship with
Austin.

The portrait of an assiduous Vinnie busily checking
boundaries in the moonlight was refuted by Vinnie herself
when she was recalled. Yes, she admitted, she had been in
the vicinity of the Todd house one winter evening, but she
had not inspected any boundaries and had most certainly
not been alone:

> I never in the evening or at any time, examined the bounds of
> that lot by walking back and forth upon the land. I never at
> any time went out anywhere alone at nine o'clock in the
> evening. I did not go from that lot into Prof. Todd's house at
> any time in December 1895, nor at any time. I don't remem-
> ber having any talk with Prof. David P. Todd or Mrs. Todd in
> their house in December, 1895, relative to the bounds of this
> particular lot. . . . My maid Margaret and I were walking one
> moonlight evening, I don't remember just when it was, and
> as we went through the street in which their house lies
> Maggie asked me if that was . . . [unexplained ellipsis in the
> original]. She asked me just where it was. My attention was
> called to the lot where the shrubbery was at the time. We

neither of us left the sidewalk or went upon the lot. I had always noticed the telegraph pole. I knew where it was. I did not at any time before the time I was with Maggie, go to the edge of the lot, or near it, for the purpose of any examination of it.

While Vinnie was on the stand, Taft took the opportunity to reinforce her previously stated recollection of the February visit, how it had not been arranged beforehand but had come to her as a pleasant surprise. "I was just going out," she explained, "and had on my wraps, and I heard the bell, and I just threw them off and went to the door, and I believe I said, as I often say when persons come and I am about to go out, 'You almost lost me.' . . . I was glad to see them and was very glad I hadn't gone out. I was just going to my brother's." That claim she repeated several times under cross-examination, adding firmly that so far as she had been aware that night, "Mr. Spaulding had no other purpose than a social call."

Timothy Spaulding took the stand at the opening of the second day's proceedings, and there was general expectation that his testimony would be decisive, naturally in the Todds' favor. But Spaulding's replies, curiously rambling and imprecise, were a disappointment. The two critical questions—had the visit been by appointment or not? Had Vinnie been fully aware that her signature to the "paper" gave away actual ownership of the strip?—were both left murkily unclear at the finish:

Miss Dickinson herself came to the door. Mrs. Todd introduced me to her, and we went into a room, I think it was the library, a room on the right of the hall as you enter, as I remember it now, and we had a long conversation there on all sorts of matters. . . . After half an hour or three-quarters of

an hour . . . Mrs. Todd produced this unsigned deed . . . and
she turned to Miss Dickinson and said,—I think she used the
word "Lavinia,"—"I have brought with me the paper we
talked about which you are to sign," and she handed it to me.
I took it up in my hands, and I read the description through
to myself. Then I turned and said, "Miss Dickinson, this
appears to be a deed of land, a deed of a piece of land
adjoining where Mrs. Todd lives, from you to Mrs. Todd,"
and I then took the deed and I gave the side lines, the dis-
tances in the deed, and the width as appeared in the deed, but
I did not read the description verbatim, simply cited the side
lines as appear here. . . .

. . . And she said, "Yes, we have talked that over before,"
and she said, "There is no hurry about this, is there?" And
Mrs. Todd said, "Mr. Spaulding is a justice of the peace, he is
over here, and now is a good time to do it." I don't know but
she said, "Now is the best time to do it," used some phrase of
that sort.

And I said, "If you are ready to do it, and willingly, and
thoroughly understand it, there is no reason why it should
not be done now as well as at any time." She said, "O, I
understand it all right, we have talked it over before. Where
am I to sign?" I put my finger on the line, and said, "On the
line beside the seal," putting my finger there. She sat at the
table and signed the deed, and I asked her if she acknowledged this as her free act and deed, and she said yes, and I
took up the pen she laid down and wrote my name as witness. . . . When she signed and I signed as witness she began
to speak of other things . . . she called our attention, to some
furniture. Possibly it was a secretary, writing-case, or some
piece of furniture which she called on us to see, and we talked
about that, and went to look at it, and we were there some
time after the deed was executed. . . .

I think the deed was produced in a room where there was a
large table of some kind, I guess we went from the library
into the dining-room. There was a set of blue china in the

dining-room. There was a lull in the conversation during
some parts of the time while the deed was being executed. . . . I think there was some conversation between her
and Mrs. Todd while we were executing it.

Asked in cross-examination to comment directly on Mabel's
claim that the visit was by appointment, Spaulding gave the
impression of being suddenly, and badly, undecided:

The earlier part of the visit was what might be called a social
call—nothing else. There was nothing said to indicate that I
came there by appointment until the matter was broached.
Nothing whatever was said about it. We were talking of entirely outside matters. Nothing whatever was said about it
that I came there at the request of Miss Dickinson for the purpose of transacting this business. I don't think there was anything that gave that notion to her mind. I don't think that any
allusion was made to the business in any way, nothing whatever. I can't answer whether anything had ever been said to me
by Mrs. Todd that this was an appointment desired by Miss
Dickinson. I don't know just about that. It seems as if she did,
as if something was said, but it is not entirely a matter of recollection. It is more a matter of argument.

At the conclusion of Spaulding's cross-examination there
was an exchange which must have proved particularly
harmful to the Todds' case. Brief though it is, it managed to
create a strong impression that the notary himself was not
entirely sure that Vinnie knew she was signing away her
land. Where and under what circumstances the "conversation" he cites took place are matters now untraceable:

Q. Have you said in conversation that, "Take women of this
   kind, that very likely one of them might be thinking of
   one sort of paper and the other thinking of another?"
A. No, not exactly that.

Unaccountably, the lawyer failed to press Spaulding for what he did say, exactly, and why he said it, and the notary's appearance concluded with his explanation of why the deed had not been properly registered. Noticeable is his certainty that fear of Sue's reaction was shared by both Mabel and Vinnie:

Mrs. Todd gave a reason for delaying registration. We were going toward her house from Miss Dickinson's. There was some conversation; something was said to me as to whether I heard what Miss Dickinson said. It began from that. I could give the reason that she gave, perhaps, without going into it. She said this, that she wanted it delayed, the recording of it held back, because Mrs. Austin Dickinson and she were estranged, there was a good deal of feeling between them, and Mrs. Austin Dickinson would make it uncomfortable for Lavinia; that is the word she used; and that on that account she wanted it, the record of it, delayed. I asked her what good that would do. I didn't see what advantage that was. Mrs. Austin Dickinson would make it unpleasant. I don't know as you want me to say anything more about it. She didn't say that Miss Dickinson assigned that reason. She said Miss Dickinson didn't want to have her record it; asked me if I heard it, and I said no, and then she gave that reason why she didn't want it herself. I understood it to be her reason. "If Mrs. Austin Dickinson discovered it was deeded to me she would make trouble, there would be a row, she wouldn't like it."

To offset Spaulding's unexpectedly weak testimony, the Todds had ready the strong witness of Vinnie's longtime neighbors Dwight Hills and his housekeeper, Mrs. Seelye. Both insisted that Vinnie had repeatedly talked with them of giving the land to Mabel and her husband, had even confessed that her mind was made up to do it. Hills's lengthy deposition was read to the court in its entirety, of which only a portion is needed here:

> She spoke to me first on the evening of her brother's death. She said, as near as I can recollect, "I shall want to turn to you for some advice." . . . it was in the very next conversation I had with her that she said, "Austin has for a long time wished me to do something for the Todds; he wanted they should have the meadow." I asked her if she had signed any agreement to do anything of that kind. She answered no. She pressed me quite hard to advise her, and I declined. I told her she must do as she thought best. I told her that I should have to ask her not to sign any paper, or agreement, without my knowledge, or examination, and she said, "most assuredly I shall not." . . . She spoke of the conveyance of this meadow land a good number of times, for three or four months. I can't tell how many. I remember once of telling her, if she had decided to give them a deed I would attend to it and get the papers made and bring the justice or witness. . . . Miss Dickinson never told me that she intended to make such a deed. She assured me that she would sign no deed, nor agreement, without my knowledge, as before stated, but not otherwise. I stopped advising her as soon as possible when I saw the notice of the deed in the "Banker and Tradesman."

Not that it's particularly relevant, but Hills is here concealing his own much wider knowledge of the situation, for as Austin's closest friend he knew all about the affair with Mabel and its family ramifications. This explains the implicit contradiction in the deposition between Hills's agreeing to advise Vinnie, then declining to do so when she "pressed me quite hard" about the land.

Immediately after the reading of the Hills deposition Mrs. Seelye was called to the stand, and she unflinchingly corroborated everything Hills had said. She also declared that she was present more than once in the Hills home when Vinnie and her employer exchanged earnest conversation on the topic of the Todds and the land. Her gossipy tone in relating one instance of overhearing the talk leaves a strong impression of its reality:

> It was in Mr. Hills' room. He was up there sick. I wasn't in the room with them while they were talking, for I knew what they were going to talk about, and I didn't suppose they would want me. I was back and forth in the hall, and went several times into the room and told her she was staying too long, he was getting tired, and finally I said so, and told her she must go. As we stood in the door to go Mr. Hills said, "When you get ready to do that I want to see that deed and see that it is all right." I didn't hear what they were talking about before that, I wasn't listening. I was part of the time in my own room on the opposite side. It is a large hall. When she came out of the room she told me what they had been talking about.

Mrs. Seelye concluded her direct testimony by insisting that Vinnie "never said anything" about promising the Todds to prohibit building on the strip. Cross-examination of the woman was lengthy, but the result was only to reinforce what she had said about Vinnie and the land and specifically that Vinnie had made up her mind to go ahead.

As the trial drew to a close with the calling of Vinnie's servant Maggie Maher, a last surprise was in store for the spectators. Since Maggie had accompanied Vinnie on that moonlight walk past the Todd place, it was expected that the trusted servant would be able to give solid support to her mistress's claim about the doings that night. But the trial record dismisses Maggie with one bare line, the rather strange comment that she provided "no material testimony." What questions were put to her by Vinnie's lawyers, whether she was cross-examined by the other side, do not appear. Some reason is needed to account for so irregular a hiatus, and once more it is seen that fear of scandal has played its unacknowledged part. The year before, when Maggie thought she would have to leave Massachusetts for a time on a family matter, she too had made a deposition. In it she referred openly to the close friendship between Mabel and Austin, saying that the two had often enjoyed long meetings behind closed doors at the Mansion and that they frequently went off together for picnics and carriage rides. By the time of the trial Maggie's personal plans had changed, and probably there was a quick agreement between the sides not to press her too closely when she took the stand (though why she was asked to testify at all remains a question).

Summation on both sides, with each attorney making detailed use of the testimony, was effective, but the abler performance, according to the newspapers, was delivered by Vinnie's advocate, S. S. Taft. Predictably he began by insisting on the marked difference observable between the litigants. Vinnie he depicted as a sheltered innocent living a life of "refinement and seclusion," in contrast to the much younger Mabel, whom he labeled as worldly and informed. Vinnie's "quiet, sincere, consistent, and convincing manner" on the witness stand he compared with Mabel's "swift and argumentative" responses, which he said left the impression that she was testifying contentiously "and not simply from recollection." Patiently he set forth his view of how the sophisticated defendant had lied to and imposed on his naive client. Spaulding's shaky testimony he handled adroitly, emphasizing the man's near-admission that Vinnie might well have been confused about the nature of the document she signed.

The Todds' attorney, John O'Donnell, in his summation

concentrated on the statements of Dwight Hills and his housekeeper, as well as the total lack of support for Vinnie's claim that she meant only to prohibit building on the strip. He stressed the correctness of Spaulding's professional conduct in making everything clear to Vinnie before the signing, and insisted there could have been no possible confusion in her mind. Three independent witnesses "of unimpeachable character," he reminded the court, had spoken for his client, where Vinnie had been unable to gather one. Cleverly, he reserved for his close a disturbing thought which he well knew had lain in the minds of his hearers since the start of the trial. Upon such weak grounds as Miss Dickinson's testimony, he said, the court is asked to believe

> that a long-time professor of Amherst College, known and distinguished throughout the scientific world for his attainments as an astronomer, and his wife, almost as widely known as himself, have conspired together to defraud this plaintiff, and have stooped to practice a criminal deception upon her in order to obtain this paltry strip of land worth five or six hundred dollars. This imputation wounds more deeply than any pecuniary loss could do.

Six weeks later—not an undue length of time—the judge's verdict was ready. It agreed with what the newspapers, citing in particular Spaulding's failure to convince, had been predicting. Without qualification, Judge John Hopkins found in Vinnie's favor: "It is ordered, adjudged and decreed that the plaintiff is entitled to the relief that she seeks." He also ordered that the Todds should pay all costs and that they must within thirty days release the disputed property back to Vinnie.

Nothing was said in the verdict about whether actual fraud had been committed, only that Vinnie was entitled to return of the land. Implicitly it was a finding that recognized the one fact too liable to be obscured: all that mattered was the one particular night in question, whether Vinnie on *that* night had or had not intended to sign a deed conveying ownership of land. This was wholly aside from the question of whether she had ever talked or thought of doing so. Had she, on *that* night, meant to give the land away? Hopkins found that she had not, but had acted out of confusion. Deliberately, it seems, he refrained from speculating as to what might have been the cause of the confusion.

*   *   *

FAILING THE DISCOVERY of new evidence, no amount of ingenuity can prove, in anything like a legal sense, what actions and motives may have been at work in the quiet of the Dickinson house on February 7, 1896. Something less than absolute proof may at times be acceptable, however, particularly in a simple review of lives long past. If so, then it may be said that sufficient evidence is now available for uncovering the probable truth of what took place that evening. As might be expected, the reality is considerably more tangled than has been thought.

In all the welter of charge and countercharge at the trial, one indisputable fact stands out: the inexperienced Vinnie did *not* consult with the man she had gratefully chosen after her brother's death to be her adviser, never spoke with him even in passing about allowing no building on the strip. Her reason for the omission, as she expressed it on the witness stand, was that she "did not consider it of any consequence. I did not consider it anything legal. It was simply a promise of friendship." Sheltered, Vinnie's life may have been, but hardly to the extent that she viewed the signing of an official document (a standard printed form), bearing the state seal and requiring the signature of a witness called in from a neighboring town, to be a casual, nonlegal act between good friends. Vinnie knew very well what she was signing that night, knew that the paper was a deed conveying land, so the reason she gave under cross-examination for avoiding Hills's offer to "attend to it and get the papers made and bring the justice" is palpably untrue. It must be that she had some other, less obvious reason for bypassing her friend's offer, and judging by what happened later, at least part of that reason may be suggested: Vinnie did not call on Hills's services because she knew that his authoritative presence would have made the transaction impossible to repudiate. In other words, it very much appears that Vinnie from the start planned to do what she eventually did.

As early as the fall of 1887 Austin had determined to bequeath Mabel his personal share of the estate he had inherited from his father (a considerable sum involving stocks, bonds, and a third interest in the Mansion and its property). But such a bequest could not, he knew, be made a part of his formal will without inviting opposition from Sue. Instead, he arranged to leave it to Vinnie, "with the request that she shall turn it over to you," as he told Mabel, adding that "she has promised to do this." After Austin's death in August 1895 seven weeks passed before Mabel raised the subject of the bequest with Vinnie, and then it brought her only a rude shock. On October 6—while she was in the midst of preparing the manuscript of Emily's third volume of poems—she dropped in at the Mansion, apparently for the purpose of claiming her inheritance. That night she wrote dejectedly in her diary, "I find she is going to ignore Austin's request to her—that she shall give me his share of his father's estate. She is, as he always told me, utterly slippery and treacherous, but he did not think she would fail to do as he stipulated in this. Oh, it is pitiful!"

With that unlooked-for development in mind, several

other occurrences, just before and just after the fateful night of February 7, 1896, may be cited. Particular note should be taken of the dates, the first of which occurs at a time when the completed manuscript of Emily's third volume had been ready for some days or weeks.

29 December 1895: Mabel notes in her diary: "I went to see Vinnie just before tea, and had a talk with her. She is going to do one lovely thing."

31 December 1895: Mabel writes to Roberts Brothers: "I send you today by express the MS of a Third Series of Emily Dickinson's *Poems.*"

7 January 1896: Mabel again writes Roberts Brothers: "I am glad to hear that the E. D. Poems can go right through at once. . . . I have said nothing to Lavinia about contracts, I will see her soon."

15 January 1896: The proofs of *Poems, Third Series* arrive in Amherst, and Mabel begins work on them.

28 January 1896: Mrs. Todd in Boston confers with Roberts Brothers about the contract for *Poems, Third Series.*

7 February 1896: Mr. Spaulding and Mrs. Todd pay a call on Vinnie, who signs the deed for the strip of land.

19 February 1896: Mabel notes in her diary: "Wrote *Preface* to E.D. Third Series, and sent off proof, plates, and Contents proof."

Is it too much to see cause and effect in this dovetailing of events, the probability that an angry Mabel forced from Vinnie a concession about Austin's indirect bequest by threatening to interrupt or impede publication of Emily's poems? Say that there was a confrontation between the two on December 29, of course of a suitably refined sort. Say the cornered Vinnie that evening agreed to do "one lovely thing," give Mabel at least the strip of land beside her house. Satisfied to get even that much, two days later Mabel sent the manuscript of *Poems, Third Series* off to the publisher in Boston. But all during January the anxious, resentful Vinnie, confused and concerned about the contract for the poems, and preparation of the volume, by one excuse or another kept putting off fulfillment of her promise. From the trial testimony, it does seem certain that she was indeed surprised to have the impatient Mabel turn up on the night of February 7, and with an official witness in tow. So concerning this aspect of the case, strangely enough, it does seem that Vinnie was telling the literal truth. But even as her guests entered the house, of one fact she was acutely aware: Mabel at that moment still had in her possession the manuscript and all the corrected proofs of Emily's third volume.

Chattering amiably about antique chairs and blue china, hardly listening to the explanations of the earnest Spaulding, but fully prepared with the story she would later tell the court about how she mistook the document, Vinnie picked up the pen and unconcernedly signed the deed.

8

Mabel's Victory

B Y THE TURN of the century, of all who had inhabited the two Dickinson houses, only Susan and her daughter remained. Ned, at age thirty-seven, with his epilepsy apparently in remission and engaged to be married, died of heart failure in May 1898. In August the next year, the aging Vinnie followed him, also a victim of heart trouble. After Vinnie's death, for another dozen years Sue lingered on, her health gradually worsening but delighting in her daughter's growing reputation as both novelist and poet. Then, on the morning of May 12, 1913, after a long illness Sue's own weakened heart gave out. "She was a woman of strong character," said the *Amherst Record* in its obituary, "and of gracious personality, and [she] gained a wide acquaintance with men and women of distinction in the world of literature and affairs." With this estimate the *Springfield Republican* agreed, saying that Mrs. Dickinson was a woman "of rare quality. . . . She possessed a charming and gracious personality, and unusual gifts as a conversationalist." Now for Martha Dickinson, deserted by her husband and not yet having filed for divorce, there began her own often solitary thirty-year vigil at the Evergreens.

Mabel Todd also noted Sue's passing. Completely severed from all contact with the Dickinsons for fifteen years, and living with her husband at the other end of town, the day after Sue's death she made an entry in her diary that showed time had brought no mellowing. In a further burst of self-delusion she wrote: "Poor old Susan died last night. A very curious nature full of (originally) fine powers most cruelly perverted. She has done incalculable evil, and wrought endless unhappiness. At times she seemed possessed of a devil—yet could be smoothly winning and interesting. Close to the surface was always the Tartar." In truth the entry provides chilly reading, for it may in full justice be taken as a first impulsive sketch of that distorted portrait of Susan that would become fixed in the minds of two generations of unsuspecting Dickinson scholars. It is a portrait conjured up by Mabel Todd alone, later aided by her dutiful daughter, Millicent, and which has now become almost ineradicable. Without at least partial rejection of the otherwise fine and dedicated work of many sincere scholars, the truth about Susan, and therefore in some part about Emily herself, must continue flawed.

Before looking at the patient way in which Mabel accomplished her purpose, it may be well to set down a rather strange, not to say revealing, incident that followed Susan's death, and which in its own way perhaps helped to stiffen Mabel's resolve against her old adversary. On the other hand, it may only mean that even Mabel had a conscience.

Immediately on hearing of Susan's death, Mabel felt, as she said later, that she had been freed of the woman's "unchanging hatred." From that day she existed "freer in my mind and occupations . . . much more completely myself than before." Six weeks afterward, on a particularly hot afternoon in July, as she walked alone to the college for a swim in the pool, suddenly from nowhere she felt "an unfriendly push or hand laying-on which startled me." At that same instant she was aware of "the hatred of some nearby influence . . . being exercised against me." Though shaken, she continued to the college and took her swim in the deserted pool, but on leaving the water, she collapsed and lay unconscious for half an hour. Found and taken to the doctor, she was told she had apparently suffered a severe heat stroke. During the many bedridden weeks that followed, as she admitted, she often "thought of Sue and her possible power to injure me," but was no longer worried because "I knew for certain she had no further power to hurt me, as she had exercised her power against me in one fierce stroke not again available." In her mind there was not the slightest doubt that a malignant, ghostly Susan "had stricken me in her pleasure to be able to work her will upon me."

It was no minor or temporary fright that Mabel felt. Probably the most surprising aspect of the whole incident is the fact that her unquestioning account of Susan's ghostly attack was written nearly twenty years after the fact, by which time the trouble had long been diagnosed as a cerebral hemorrhage.

★   ★   ★

AFTER SUFFERING ECLIPSE for more than twenty years following its rapid rise in the early nineties, Emily Dickinson's reputation began its recovery just as the centenary of her birth, due in 1930, approached. With serious interest in her life and writings steadily building, the circumstance that her original editor from the nineties still lived—the same Mrs. Todd who since the start had been accepted as the leading authority on Emily, and on everything connected with the Dickinsons—was seen by hopeful critics and biographers as a marvelous opportunity. Two of these in

particular, Josephine Pollitt and Genevieve Taggard, made a
direct appeal for assistance, and each was warmly welcomed
by Mrs. Todd. Books by both women—able enthusiasts
rather than serious scholars—appeared in the year of the
centenary and were well received, Taggard's reaching a
fourth printing that same year. In neither volume was anything seen amiss at the time, but it is now clear that while
Mabel succeeded in imposing her view of Susan on only one
of the two, that single success established the tone and
direction of much that was to come.

   As it happened, it was the experienced but trusting Taggard, a published poet in her own right, who was caught,
and not Miss Pollitt, a young graduate student when she
first applied to Mabel. Accepting without evidence and
without demur all that Mabel told her, Taggard found that
Sue's role in Emily's life had been a severe disappointment.
At first, wrote Taggard, Emily admired Susan as a
"Heaven-sent" friend and ally, but before long her sister-in-
law's deficiencies intruded:

> Sue proved to be a blind alley . . . finally, for some reason not
> shown, in spite of affectionate notes and protestations to the
> end, Sue was simply not alive in Emily's heart. . . . We sus-
> pect that Sue shared to some extent the town view of Emily
> . . . she was a little hard and what of worldly inclination
> appeared as a merit when [Sue] was young, became, when
> she grew older, not a merit, but for Emily, who was swinging
> far away from the world as she passed thirty, something of a
> defect . . . scintillation was a sickness in Sue. . . . For some
> reason, probably originating in temperament, Sue gave Em-
> ily no way of escape and very little nourishment in spite of the
> books she brought her.

With that bare assertion, for which she cites no source, the
innocent Taggard at a stroke deprived Sue of her rightful

place as Emily's lifelong friend and only true confidante. Mabel Todd's campaign had begun.

At the same time, Mabel began weaving what was to become another strand in her tangled web, this time persuading both Pollitt and Taggard that it was she who had been Emily's true favorite: having dismissed Sue from the post of honor, she moved quickly to fill the place herself. "Mrs. Todd," wrote Pollitt, echoing Mabel faithfully, "apprehended the nature of the brilliant and secluded Amherst poet as few did at that time," and she soon became one of "the few who could be termed an intimate friend, one of those whom Emily personally received." In different ways that spurious claim was to appear in most of the subsequent writing on Emily, its falsity long going undetected. While never quite making an outright statement that she had ever actually been face-to-face with the poet, Mabel still managed to give the undoubted impression that she had repeatedly enjoyed exactly that privilege. A comment from one of her own lectures on Emily, quoted by Taggard from a listener's notes, shows how careful she was in this respect: "Mrs. Todd was one of the comparatively few who were admitted to anything like intimacy with the weird recluse of Amherst," though she had never "in all the years of her acquaintance with her had a face-to-face conversation about commonplace, mundane affairs." But some measure of pity and even indulgence may be in order here. From the start Mabel was in the impossible position of having to admit publicly that her years of supposed close friendship with the poet had not earned her even a single meeting. Allowing a deftly constructed lie to circulate nicely solved the problem.

The second innocent victim of Mabel's campaign proved to be the respected professional scholar and critic George Whicher of Amherst College. Though he produced the first authoritative account of Emily's life and career—really a

thoroughly satisfying book that in other respects was a fine
and sensitive pioneer performance—in the lesser area of
Emily's relations with Sue, Whicher completely lost his
footing. So well did Mabel indoctrinate him that he could
actually, in a "Bibliographical Postscript," make the following admission, which must be unique in an experienced
scholar: "It should be clearly stated that I have not asked or
received aid from any surviving member of the Dickinson
family [meaning Martha]. Whether this independence is
considered an advantage or a disadvantage to a biographer
of Emily Dickinson will depend on one's point of view. I am
inclined to value it." This, of course, is equivalent to a
biographer of Shelley loftily refusing to consult Medwin or
Trelawney, a Wordsworth scholar ignoring Poole.

   After that bald admission it is certainly no surprise to find
that Whicher's opinion of Susan Dickinson not only agrees
with that of Taggard but expands on it. Austin's marriage, he
states, expressing his belief roundly as if it were a mere fact,

> brought into the closely knit Dickinson family an alien and
> dazzling personality. Susan . . . possessed a quick mind and a
> superficially opulent nature. As the daughter of a village
> tavernkeeper, she had been early touched by worldly influ-
> ences . . . her wit was ruthless. . . . Those who knew her only
> as a vivacious hostess have left abundant testimonies to her
> charm. Between public appearances her charm was less nota-
> ble. . . .
>
> Austin, like Emily, was at first fascinated by his lady's
> gaiety and freedom, but in the end he reverted to a strong
> preference for a more Puritan mentality.* . . . The profound
> alienation that separated Austin from his wife and his two
> eldest children is important only in its bearing on the life of
> Emily Dickinson. Both Emily and Lavinia were unques-

---

* Does this phrase prove, or not, that Whicher was ignorant of Austin's
adultery? It's hard to be sure.

tionably loyal to their brother. . . . There was no open break
but for weeks at a time intercourse between the two sisters-
in-law was suspended. Sue was no doubt busy with scintilla-
tion, and Emily had her poems to attend to. Insensibly they
drifted further and further apart.

Living in Amherst as he did, his position on the college
faculty giving him access to all inside circles, did Whicher
never pick up even faint echoes of that far-off period when
Mabel and Austin were the town scandal? Did he never
suspect that the illicit affair might itself be enough to explain what he calls the "profound alienation" between Sue
and her husband, also explaining much else in Emily's own
story? Apparently he didn't. Instead, he offered what purport to be his proofs for the claim of long alienation. They
are three: 1) the fact that Sue "betrayed" Emily by giving
one of her poems to a newspaper, 2) the phrase *pseudo-sister*
as a punning reference to Sue in a letter of Emily's, 3)
another note of Emily's stating that except for Shakespeare,
Sue had given her the most knowledge of life. That, liter-
ally, is the extent of Whicher's evidence, though the three
items are wrapped in deft covering phrases, such as "signs
of strain are only too evident," and the old reliable "the
word speaks volumes."

Whicher was the last to be influenced by Mabel directly
and in person, for she died in October 1932. But her daughter, Millicent, then married and in her early fifties, immediately took up the task. Without any pang of conscience,
seemingly, she made her first and most important decision,
that her mother's affair with Austin should continue to be a
secret. Whether she did so on orders from, or by suggestion
of, her mother is now an unanswerable if nagging question,
but either way, for almost another forty years, while Dickinson interest became epidemic, Millicent held her tongue,

somehow managing to persuade herself that the affair itself was not relevant. In her several writings she strove to give an impression of honest, sincere endeavor ("Facts no longer need be glossed over or evaded," etc.), yet she was promulgating what amounted to a massive lie.

Millicent's first publication was the volume *Ancestors' Brocades: The Literary Debut of Emily Dickinson*. It had been begun in collaboration with her mother, and Mabel's death brought small interruption, for the work was ready for publication as early as 1935. For a variety of reasons it was kept back, chief among them being Martha Dickinson's inconvenient presence on the scene—or as Millicent preferred to put it, "Susan's daughter was still living, and the book was frank." The way was cleared at last by Martha's death in 1943, but then the war interfered, and it was not until 1945 that the volume finally made its appearance. Besides greatly elevating Mabel's role in the rescue of Emily's poetry, it added a devastating touch to the picture of Susan as the worldly, destructive "alien" in the Dickinson circle.

Two sorts of distortion are detectable, the main strand concerning Sue personally, and another touching on her later strained relations with Vinnie. This undoubted falling-out between Sue and Vinnie in the late 1890s is steadily pursued, of course with full blame being laid to Sue's own shortcomings. The truth of the matter, that the antagonism between the sisters-in-law began only as Vinnie took Mabel's side in the love affair, and worsened when Sue found that the despised Mrs. Todd had become Emily's editor, goes unmentioned. Millicent, it is certain, was well aware of the truth but could take no chance on submitting her mother's character to public scrutiny.

Besides many deprecatory allusions of a more minor sort, the one sustained comment on Sue in *Ancestors' Brocades* links Millicent directly and knowingly to the blatant impositions of Taggard and Whicher. Especially unfortunate in the passage is a new note in the campaign, her slighting innuendo about Sue's father. Even as she wrote the words, in her files lay evidence to the contrary:

> From the few allusions made to Austin's wife thus far the reader may not have gained a very clear impression of her. It is not for me to dissect Sue's character, but her relationship to Emily is an essential part of our story. In view of their fundamentally opposite attitudes toward life, the lifelong intimacy depicted by Sue's daughter is hard to believe.
>
> Sue was a product of the Connecticut Valley. Her father, Thomas Gilbert, presided successively over hostelries in Greenfield, in Deerfield, and for a few years in Amherst, where in 1832 he leased the Mansion House, a tavern and a livery-stable not far from the Dickinson property. For the next five years he and his family lived in Amherst where his convivial habits were well known. . . .
>
> As a girl Sue had a lush personality which charmed Emily and Vinnie. They were enthusiastic over her marriage to their brother, deluging her with expressions of affection. But not long after her marriage to the catch of the town she began to take on the airs of a great lady. . . . She assumed an attitude of lofty aloofness scarcely deigning, as she drove about town in her barouche, to acknowledge the greetings of her former schoolmates . . . pretense and pose came to be her most noticeable characteristics. . . .
>
> Emily grieved. For of all her friends Sue had the liveliest mind—one which gave promise of real and lasting companionship and understanding. But she seemed to care only for appearances. While Emily was plumbing the depths of creation, Sue next door was busy with "scintillation" at the expense of her friends.

Those "convivial habits" of Sue's father soon became, in Dickinson biography, first habitual drunkenness and then

the specific cause of his death in 1841. In the end, the habit
was even transferred to Sue herself. But as early as 1930 the
two Todd women had quietly commissioned a search of the
Greenfield records on Thomas Gilbert. In his youth, the
researcher found, he had served his country well as a soldier
in the War of 1812, and later, in addition to being a pros-
perous tavernkeeper, had held several elective offices. "I
have failed to find anything anywhere," reported the researcher, "that was of an adverse nature to an upright character." No hint of that search or its results appeared
anywhere until years after Millicent's death.

Ancestors' Brocades also supplied another, and rather startling element in the denigration of Susan. Strongly it suggested that her various "cruelties" not only had helped bring
about Vinnie's death but had actually hastened Emily's.
This it accomplished by simply quoting from some personal
letters that had reached the Todd women about 1930 from a
former Amherst resident, Mary Lee Hall. As a young
nurse, then lately arrived in Amherst, Hall had become
friendly with the lonely, aging Vinnie, and now—some
forty years later—it appeared she had a story to tell. Millicent, never doubting the woman's competence, allowed her
to tell it in extracts from the letters that spread over four
pages in *Ancestors' Brocades*. Of these extracts, three are
sufficient to show how Sue's memory was further blithely
impugned:

> . . . after Ned's death, Vinnie asked me to copy [Emily's
> poems] and help her to have them published. . . . I copied
> many of them, and intended helping Vinnie to do as she
> wished me to, but there was "war between the houses" espe-
> cially severe, and so much was done to cruelly hurt Vinnie
> that she became seriously ill. . . .

> . . . Vinnie was not well all winter and was not up during

the summer (1899)—it was "the Dickinson heart" as she called it. . . . The cause of her last illness was Sue who terrified her and treated her shamefully [two instances are given of Sue's harassment of Vinnie: she had her gardener take manure without permission from Vinnie's barn, and she sent her dog to the Mansion, where "he worried the pussies"]. . . .

. . . [Vinnie] told me Sue had been cruel to Emily and herself and they each had suffered keenly from her insincerities, her insane jealousies, as well as her intentional deceit. Vinnie often said that Emily's life was shortened by at least ten years by Sue's cruel treatment. I know that Vinnie told Mrs. Stockbridge that Sue never ceased to annoy her in every possible way, and that she felt she was trying to kill her as she knew her heart was weak.

Since Miss Hall makes a second appearance in the somber drama, at this point no more need be said of her testimony than this: Mary Hall, who never married, did not arrive in Amherst until 1885 at the earliest, was not befriended by Vinnie until some years afterward, and was gone from Amherst by 1904. In reality she was—some plain if uncharitable language is necessary here—the very model of an interfering busybody, a wide-eyed gossip who assumed she knew a great deal more about the Dickinsons than she actually did.

Soon after finishing *Ancestors' Brocades*, Millicent turned to preparation of still another book based on her mother's hoard of Dickinson papers. The result, in final form by 1950, was *Emily Dickinson's Home: Letters of Edward Dickinson and His Family, with Documentation and Comment*. In this account, which closes with the death of Mr. Dickinson in 1874, Sue as Austin's wife necessarily has a part. But inevitably it becomes the identical role assigned her by Mabel years before, that of the unloved wife. Even in the Preface,

Austin's married life is termed a "tragedy," and in the text itself there are several casual asides on his "domestic tribulation," along with more than a hint that Sue had managed to snare him despite his strong preference for her younger sister. Knowing the truth as she did of her own mother's behavior, Millicent could hardly have written the following passage without a severe wrench to her conscience:

> Nor had Austin foreseen another deep shadow: a lack of mutual understanding with his wife. . . . Without further elaboration at this point, it may be enough to say that it was due to conflicting aims and fundamentally different ideals. The estrangement between Austin and Sue which became apparent not long after their marriage widened with the years. . . . Austin was to find himself more and more a stranger beneath his own roof.

The key to the passage, of course, lies in that phrase "not long after their marriage." If it could be established that the Dickinson marriage had early gone on the rocks, right at the beginning, there would be no pressing need to bring in all that unpleasant business about Mabel's adultery. The same assertion about early marital strife would also tend greatly to lessen Mabel's guilt, if and when the true facts did surface.

By simply saying it was so, lacking any real proof, Taggard, Whicher, and Millicent (by then Mrs. Bingham) were able to fasten on Dickinson scholarship the Todd version of Sue's story, mainly the early loss of her husband's love and later that of her poet friend. For the next twenty years, in book after book dealing with Emily and her circle, Sue's grievous faults and "alien" nature become standard fare, recited quite matter-of-factly. More concerned about Emily's poems and about the puzzle of her artistic

development—understandably, let it be said—no commentator paused to inquire as to the grounds of the serious
charges laid against the long-dead Mrs. Dickinson. The
tendency, indeed, was just to the opposite, Sue becoming
fair game for all sorts of additional inferences. "She had a
grief of origin," typically wrote one scholar in 1967, who
acknowledges a debt to Mrs. Bingham. There were, he
explained, "memories of a tavern-keeper father who died an
alcoholic, of life as an orphan shunted from one relative to
another. Along the way ambition replaced love. Sue must
shine . . . she must live on a scale of extravagance which kept
Austin continually worried about money. . . . It was this
incapacity [to love] which gradually darkened her life and
the lives of all the Dickinsons." For all this, again typically,
no evidence whatever is supplied.

Mrs. Bingham died in December 1968, aged eighty-
eight. Long before that, however, she had made arrangements to have the full story of "her mother's involvement"
in the Dickinson saga told. Well aware that it would be a
formidable task, she chose with great care and foresight, as
early as 1946 broaching the topic of a book to the young but
respected Yale scholar Richard Sewall. "Ten years later,"
wrote Sewall afterward, somewhat cryptically, "she gave
me the first full view of its possible dimensions; and shortly
after that her papers, indispensable to the project, came to
Yale. . . . She tied no strings and asked for no prior commit-
ments." Her real concern, as she explained it to the Yale
scholar, was not with her own mother. Rather, it was with
Emily, with spreading knowledge of her poetry by means of
"new documentation and the new insights it provided." She
did make one firm stipulation (apparently not a "string" in
Sewall's estimate), which was that the story of her mother's
adulterous affair must not be told separately. It was to be
included in a full-scale Dickinson biography.

During more than a decade, from about 1956 to 1968, Sewall made slow if steady progress on the book, frequently conferring with Mrs. Bingham. Five years after her death, having been nearly two decades in preparation, *The Life of Emily Dickinson*, in two volumes comprising over eight hundred pages, was published. With this there virtually disappeared any chance that the truth about Susan would survive. Somehow, as with all the others, the conscientious Sewall too had been made captive.

Meticulous and evenhanded where he treats of Emily and her artistic concerns, in dealing with the family next door Sewall disappointingly follows his predecessors. Offering no new or hard evidence, but much in the way of "probability," he fully endorses and even expands on the now-familiar portrait. A muted afterthought in which he inclines to feel that "ultimate clarity may still be far off " seems to offer momentary redemption. But that promising insight or admission, sad to say, gives him no true pause.

Sue Dickinson first makes an entrance in the Sewall biography in an early chapter devoted to Austin, and promptly the supposed incompatibility of the couple is emphasized by being pushed even further back into the long years of the marriage, in fact all the way to courtship days. The feat is accomplished not by means of outright evidence but by a species of analysis in which the jumbled drafts of Austin's youthful love letters to Sue are studied as if they were legal documents (repeat *drafts*, and just why drafts should have been kept by Austin and Sue for forty years, or by either, is a question not addressed). Conceding that there are "moments of rapture" in them, Sewall nevertheless finds the scribbled, much written-over manuscripts to be decidedly "turbulent" and revealingly full of "uncertainty" about Susan's feelings. Where other readers might see these immature missives for what they are, the overdrawn posturing of a young man in love and much impressed with his own verbal abilities (and under the spell of such popular books as the gushing *Reveries of a Bachelor*, an obvious model), Sewall is able to detect only "signs of trouble ahead."

Long before he gives any hint of Mabel Todd's part in the drama, Sewall sets about establishing by analysis of the courtship letters that the marriage of Sue and Austin was doomed from the start. The following interpretive comments all too clearly spring from hindsight:

> Always there is the sense that Austin is reaching out for more than Susan was prepared to give.

> There is little evidence Sue shared his feelings with anything like his fervor, and there is a good deal of evidence that she did not. [A truly distorted use of the word *evidence*, since there is none either way.]

> His pleading is perhaps sufficient measure of Sue's response. He was troubled by her moods, which ranged from "stately indifference" . . . to the stormy and unpredictable.

> For a young man supposedly engaged for some time, these letters show at the very least a precarious uncertainty.

> If we can trust the evidence of several letters to her brothers, Susan approached the marriage coolly and unromantically. [Again the word *evidence* is misleading].

The cap to these remarks of Sewall on the courtship days is another comment of his occurring on a later page of the biography but which properly belongs here. It concerns the admitted fact that Austin's father was very much in favor of having Susan for a daughter-in-law and had let his high opinion of her be known to all at the time. But in this, Sewall insists, Mr. Dickinson was wrong: "What Edward failed to see was that in encouraging the match between

Susan and Austin, he was inviting into the family an alien and disruptive element. This is not a moral judgment; it is simply a fact." Of course, it is by no means a fact, and what Sewall himself failed to see is that the elder Dickinson, certainly nobody's fool, might be taken as presenting some legitimate "evidence" in the matter. But this is only another instance of a convinced scholar finding precisely what he was searching for.

Taking his cue from Mrs. Bingham, Sewall next brings in the idea of Sue's younger sister's being a serious rival for Austin's affections. This is his assured comment on the fact that Austin in the end chose Sue: "In the light of what happened, it seems to have been a tragic mistake for all concerned, including Emily." More than any who preceded him, Sewall reads back into the earlier lives of all the participants the various supposed fallings-out of a later time. For him, everything that occurred in the long years prior to the arrival of Mabel Todd is to be judged by "the light of what happened" after she appeared on the scene, and often by the light of what she *says* happened. A good illustration of this occurs in his picture of the early days of the marriage, easily recognized as precisely echoing Taggard and Whicher: "Sue's temperament, tastes, and social ambition created an atmosphere in which the Dickinson qualities, at least Austin's and Emily's—given more to the creative and speculative, and requiring solitude—found less and less sustenance." It is not easy for a reader of Sewall's long and weighty book to grasp and keep in mind the fact that for all such confident assertions he offers *no* real proof and very little in the way of evidence.

Especially to be deplored is his handling of the charge regarding Sue's so-called extravagance, for he makes it, perhaps inadvertently, a strong contributing factor in Austin's death. On facing pages of his volume occur two obviously related statements, the plain import of which no attentive reader could miss. The first statement concludes a discussion of Sue's desire for social eminence in the town. The second ends what amounts to a panegyric on the hardworking Austin's busy career as town and college official and family provider:

> But for Austin, not only was Sue's "salon"—the teas, the musicales, the dancing parties (oyster stew at ten)—expensive, and for this reason alone a burden, but the whole affair rang increasingly hollow. . . .

> He once remarked to Mrs. Todd: "I have a very expensive family." Austin seriously overtaxed his strength, and it was generally agreed that his final illness was brought on by exhaustion.

There is no hint in this connection of Austin's own notorious expenditures on original oil paintings, an extravagance on his part long known, of his giving money and land to the Todds, or of the way he quite willingly taxed his strength by the emotional and physical demands of his double life.

But these things formed only the preliminary in the Sewall biography. Of even greater interest and importance was the lengthy section in which the biographer honored his commitment to Mrs. Bingham to tell her mother's story. Running fully 130 pages, the section is dramatically entitled "War Between the Houses," an unfortunate phrase picked up from the intemperate Hall letters. It will no doubt seem harsh to say so, but in many ways there exists in American literature no more peculiar or misleading a document. Its presence in the Sewall volume badly mars what is in other respects a distinguished performance.

The space of a small book would be required to analyze and untangle, or even to discuss, all the errors and distor-

tions in the Todd section of the Sewall volume, so a sam-
pling of the more serious must serve. Fittingly, the very
paragraph with which the section opens affords a prime
instance, for if it had been written by Mabel Todd herself, it
could not have been more to her liking. In it the one condition needed for her justification is stated not as possible or
probable but as received truth:

> The ill feeling between the Homestead and the Evergreens
> had its origins in personal incompatibilities that go back to
> the time of Austin's troubled courtship. . . . By Mabel Todd's
> time it had sufficiently advanced so that, at her first encoun-
> ter with the Dickinsons, she realized that she was entering "a
> family quarrel of endless involutions." By the mid-1880s
> what had heretofore been kept under cover was all but open
> warfare. . . . The quarrel by then, of course, was over Aus-
> tin, whose affair with Mabel was being talked about in town;
> but this new development served merely to exacerbate old
> animosities and widen existing gaps.

It is no surprise, after that, to find that Mabel receives from
this biographer very gentle treatment indeed, or that he is
satisfied to let his story unfold, as he says, "mainly from
Mabel Todd's records." Though he is momentarily conscious that those records might be suspect, he quickly manages to put the thought aside. Mrs. Todd, he begins, was
certainly not unbiased:

> She was every inch a participant, deeply in love with Aus-
> tin, taking his side on every issue, and (in her journals and
> letters) defending her love against the world. . . . Neverthe-
> less . . . her account is by far the most complete we have, and
> impressively detailed . . . to read her daily entries is to gain
> confidence in her respect for fact and accuracy . . . it seems to

have been her sincere purpose to record the truth as she saw it, youthful, passionate, self-centered as she may have been.

This lax attitude—strangely so for such an ordinarily sound and careful scholar—of course could not avoid giving a subtle wrench to subsequent judgments, a result to be seen at many points in Sewall's text. An example is available in what he says of the love letters Austin wrote Mabel. In these, he comments effusively, "the rhetoric soars to crescendo after crescendo," and he describes their "sustained elevation, the almost awesome fervor," all of which leads him to detect in the letter writer "a heart too long frustrated and denied." From that quick reading he is able to produce a conclusion no whit earned: "One can only conclude that his hopes for happiness with Sue, stated with such fervor in the courtship letters, had long since come to nothing." Of course, this goes much too far—only someone who was already so convinced would so conclude, so decisively. For most, even those without special knowledge of the case, Austin's love letters to a woman half his age simply tell the old, old story. Certainly they do not demonstrate that his marriage of twenty-five years had failed "long since."

A peculiar air, at many places in his text, of hesitation or diffidence shows that Sewall did indeed know fleeting doubts of the portrait he was drawing. One especially glaring instance, in which a curious confusion is evident, occurs in a statement involving only seven sentences, the sequence of which is downright spasmodic. Analysis of the seven sentences, in light of the facts, uncovers the reason for the indecision.★

After noting the arrival of the Todds in Amherst, and

★ The passage, intact, may be read in the Notes below, p. 212.

stating that they were soon "well launched" in the town's social circles, Sewall adds, "But this pleasant state of affairs did not last." Here might be expected, as the reason things didn't last, some reference to Mabel's flirtatious ways with Ned and Austin. Instead, this is what follows: "Mabel soon learned that Sue Dickinson was known in town for her violent but short-lived enthusiasms, a fate (Mabel was warned) that might befall even Sue's 'darling Toddy.'" The fault for the break, then, was not Mabel's, but is to be laid to Sue's account? Not at all: "Sue, however, was not the immediate cause of trouble." Here, surely, after going momentarily off course, Sewall will insert the truth about the coquettish Mabel? No again. It was all Ned's doing: "What led to an open break was that Ned, Austin and Sue's twenty-year-old son, in his enthusiasm over this brilliant newcomer fell in love with her." The rest of the statement shows a conscientiously "disturbed" Mabel trying in her mature way to discourage the moony youth. It also needs pointing out that neither here nor elsewhere in his text does Sewall make the reality plain, that Mabel at one point welcomed, encouraged, and played with the affections of both father and son simultaneously.

Sewall also makes use of two other very questionable documents he had obtained from Mrs. Bingham: a clutch of autobiographical manuscripts, all brief, prepared by her mother about 1930 for use in *Ancestors' Brocades*, and the original letters of Mary Lee Hall. Both of these are legitimate sources of study, though neither may be used without a high degree of informed skepticism (Mabel's manuscripts alone contain many instances of misleading innuendo, lies, and half-truths). Sewall's employment of both sources, however, is all too free and trusting. Hardly sufficient, for instance, is his brief comment about the Hall letters (in an appendix), to the effect that "Mary Lee Hall's bias is clear;

she hated Sue and was fond of Vinnie." This ignores several more pertinent facts—for example, that Hall's sprawling observations concern only the decade of the nineties and that her information about all the Dickinsons was limited to, and controlled by, what Vinnie was willing to tell her. In his main text—where the Hall bias is not mentioned—he allows Hall's unbridled statements free rein, even to depicting Sue as "evil-minded . . . a fiend," and leaving unchallenged a reference to what he himself calls—without a wisp of proof—"the local gossip about Sue's alcoholism." At last he permits Hall to introduce a new disgrace for Sue, letting stand without comment several entirely gratuitous remarks on her "questionable relationship" with family friend Sam Bowles, as well as "other" unnamed men.

Unsure and uneasy as is Sewall's touch with these things, what he has to say on the topic of Sue's friendship with Emily is even more lamentable. Taking up the much talked-of late break between the two, he admits that "the materials to go on are few and ambiguous," and he almost immediately concedes what is the truth, that "there is no clear evidence of a break." But this does not keep him from rather promptly announcing that there was indeed an "estrangement" between the women, decided and final. His conclusion is based directly on the Todd assertions, supplemented by a study of those same "ambiguous" materials, principally a close analysis of Emily's letters and poems as they relate to Sue. In building a case from this sort of analytical study it is permissible to have a certain number of the weak links of probability, always labeled as such, with qualifiers that identify the speculation. In Sewall's chapter on "Susan and Emily" (pages 197–214, with a third of the space given to quotation of the letters and the poetry), the following lengthy string of qualifying phrases threads itself quietly through the text:

May imply—may be—may have—seems beyond question—may have been—If she implies—it also seems—appears to be—may have—might imply—apparently—if all this time—may be—apparently—may relate—may be—may be—one can only suspect—may be—was probably—seems to come—suggests—may be—would seem to be—if it is so, may explain—may tell much—possibly—seems unmistakable—can be fairly sure—what looks like—may have been—seems almost unavoidable—if these resulted—if reports are true—this sequence of possibilities—may have been—might explain—is possible—if such it was—may have—may have—some such hypothesis ... seems necessary—

At how many removes from the reality, from anything resembling truth, does such determined groping stand? Shall it be allowed to displace and smother the prober's own prior admission that "there is no clear evidence of a break"? No? It already has.

Several examples, by no means extreme, of Sewall's often faulty interpretive process must close the discussion of this widely influential book.

Talking of Emily's supposedly broken link with the family at the Evergreens, he quotes what he styles a "report" (actually a passing reference in a private letter) by a neighbor, Mrs. Jameson, that up to the very night of Gilbert's death Emily had not entered the other house for fifteen years. Six pages later Mrs. Jameson's casual remark has been inflated to "the local estimate," not otherwise identified. Then after another nine pages this local estimate has suddenly and unaccountably risen to the status of "an extraordinary fact." On this shaky basis is the supposed estrangement clinched.

A second, very similar example concerns Vinnie. An entry in Mabel's diary is quoted (October 6, 1895) which asserts that Austin actually had little affection for or trust in his younger sister: "She is, as he always told me, utterly slippery and treacherous. . . . He had an entire contempt for her." On this Sewall comments that there is no evidence, "except this statement of Mabel's," that Austin thought so harshly of Vinnie. Then occurs this curiously worded paragraph of six sentences:

> One further thought suggests itself: there may have been some truth in Austin's distrust of Vinnie, even though Mabel's report of it may be extreme. If there was, then his isolation in the family circle was more complete than other evidence suggests. And did Emily share his distrust of Vinnie? Emily seems to have been the only one in the family whom he trusted completely. This final revelation about Vinnie, however ambiguous, brings Austin and Emily closer together. It is obvious where the spiritual refreshment of his daily calls on his sisters really came from.

The reasoning process here is of the same giddily meandering sort to be noted whenever Sewall is dealing with Mabel or her records. The first sentence suggests that there "may have been" some truth in Mabel's diary claim. Then follow an "if there was" and a "seems to have been," and by the time the fifth sentence is reached Mabel's doubtful claim has become a "final revelation." Note that, rather remarkably, the effect of this "revelation" is undiminished by its probably "ambiguous" nature. Note also, and especially, that Sewall's conclusion from this murky jumble of inferences has somehow in the process become "obvious."

A third example offers something of a puzzle since it is so clearly wrongheaded, a flaw not typical of this usually well-balanced scholar. In studying the strikingly original note of

sympathy that Emily sent Susan shortly after Gilbert's
death, he is quite surprised to find that Emily has deliberately withheld proper recognition of the bereaved mother.*
There is in the note, he complains, none of that personal
comfort she expressed so well in similar letters to others, for
him a significant omission. "Beautiful as the letter is, Sue,
the grieving mother, is hardly in it at all . . . there is only the
wonder and beauty of the lost child and the mystery of
death." Every writer, the present one included, looking
back on his published work finds things he would like to
alter or omit. For Sewall, let this one be forgotten (oh, that
only!).

In the long parade of special witnesses against Susan there
was one last pronouncement to come, a book that appeared
in 1984 and which would have taken even Mabel Todd by
surprise: *Austin and Mabel: The Amherst Affair and Love Letters of Austin Dickinson and Mabel Loomis Todd.* Fortunately
there is no pressing need to go through this 450-page volume (more than half the space is given to the text of the
letters) in an effort to correct its often startling excesses
about Susan. Involved are the same unsupported accusations
and wild charges heard since the start, now creatively
lengthened by addition of much hypothetical detail. Some
unfettered psychologizing also manages to lend a curious
dignity to the proceedings ("Sue hovered dominant, powerful, and potentially disruptive in Emily's awareness, a dark,
explosive aspect of the life forces the poet wrestled to control," etc.). Mabel's journals are accepted almost as models
of objective reporting, and are liberally employed to recon-
struct, as background for the letters, the progress of the
illicit affair. Emily and Vinnie—without proof—are both
stated as giving full and apparently delighted consent to

---

* For the letter in full see above, p. 69.

their brother's adultery: they were not only aware of it, "they became accessory to it." Through it all, the by-now faceless David Todd is for long stretches kept out of sight while the "incredible" love of the two principals goes forward.

In this book Sue at last becomes a pathetic figure. As a young bride she is endowed with a mortal fear of bearing children, as well as an intense aversion to the sex act (both ideas picked up from Mabel's journal). She is seen to have married only as a convenience, having much preferred several other men to Austin—who might have been happily married to her sister Martha had not Sue interfered. "It isn't hard to understand how Sue easily and often injured both Austin and Emily" is one of the book's typically loose observations, typical also in the ephemeral nature of the injuries cited.

Finally the book shows how Sue's "conflicted personality," now including such unexplained defects as "vindictiveness," earns her the total loss of Emily's friendship. The poet, her sensibilities mortally wounded by Sue's many faults—cool, cruel, selfish, and unpredictable, about sums them up—turns permanently from her old companion in "bafflement and pain." And all of this is to be accepted not on a clear evidentiary basis but because it was long ago asserted by Mabel Todd, and has been a staple belief since Taggard and Whicher.

The author-editor of *Austin and Mabel*, Polly Longsworth, began her studies in 1972 as an associate of Richard Sewall. At his invitation she worked her way, as she said, through "the rich lode of partially organized materials" at Yale, her labors supported by Sewall's "faith and enthusiasm." In her book, which does give abundant evidence of industry, there is reflected a sincere desire to find the truth. That she ended far short of that goal where Sue is concerned, simply identifies her as one more in the line of dedicated but wonderfully mesmerized scholars who have dealt with the topic. The grievously flawed Susan Dickinson who stalks so calculatingly through Longsworth's pages—as through the pages of a dozen other scholarly works—is the creation of no one but Mabel Todd. The intelligent and responsible woman who actually lived, in joy and sadness and no doubt with some share of human faults, for more than half a century at the Evergreens is no longer to be found.

The self-serving entry Mabel made in her diary on the day after Susan's death, nearly eighty years ago, has today become the standard view in Dickinson scholarship. Nor, despite all that can be said to the contrary, does it appear that it will soon be rooted out. Unless human nature has changed radically, it may be accepted that for some time to come Sue Dickinson will remain perhaps the most sadly traduced figure in American literature, a victim not really of malice but of scholarly naiveté, I will not say indifference.

Still, these are earthly things, and it is good to remember that for the thoughtful there is always another kind of consolation. Where Susan most probably is right now she may feel that the doleful record presented in these pages is worth no more than a brief, pitying sigh, if sighs have a place there.

Notes and Sources

References are given in shortened form and are easily identified by a glance at the bibliography. For quoted matter the first few words of the quotation are repeated, enough to make identification sure.

Prologue: *Gib's Room*

Just a year after my visit to the Evergreens Mrs. Hampson was found lying unconscious in the center hall of the house at the foot of the long stairway. She spent the next eighteen months in nursing homes, most of the time disoriented mentally, and died on January 5, 1988. Her will leaves the Evergreens to a trust, specifying that it be made into a cultural center.

7 "a door into the past": Bianchi, *Face*, 166.

Chapter 1: *Home Is a Holy Thing*

17 "That's the little girl": *Letters*, 751. The recipient of this note is given in *Letters* as Martha Dickinson, but it bears no salutation, and the signature is "Emily," which would not have been signed to the niece. See the facsimile of the original in Bianchi, *Face*, 178. The photograph of Martha, first published in *Letters*, 778, is in the photo section above.

19 Susan's asking about Einstein is in a letter written by President George Olds of Amherst College, quoted in Bianchi, *Face*, 145. "It was amazing," wrote Olds, "to find a woman of her

age so intelligently interested in a dream reaching to the very borderlands of scientific progress."

19   "with greedy interest": Bianchi, *Face*, 59. Same for the two other quotations in this paragraph.

19   "talked of serious": Bianchi, *Face*, 45. Same for the two other quotations in this paragraph, 31, 43.

20   "She was of medium": Bianchi, *Face*, 15, 17.

21   "a self-reliance rare": *Amherst Record*, Oct. 17, 1883.

21   "Talk of 'hoary Reprobates!' ": *Letters*, 673.

21   "his piercing cries of ": *Letters*, 585.

21   "pretty execrations": *Letters*, 916. Same for the other quotation in this paragraph.

21   "willful and winsome": Bianchi, *Face*, 172.

22   "proud—sometime": *Letters*, 380.

22   "distinguished": *Letters*, 345.

23   "a holy thing. Nothing": *Letters*, 150.

23   "A home Sue! It's too": Sewall, I, 108. Equally sad to read, in view of what happened, is another of Austin's letters on the charms of home, written in his youth: "Oh, a home, Sue, its rights and duties and beauty, all more than any word can tell. Thank God for it." Or this, also written to Sue: "How I love to picture you as my wife—the mornings when we shall sit at the same table, at the same hearth." Both letters in Bianchi, *Face*, 121.

25   "Dear Toddy, The world": unpublished. Quoted from the original in the Dickinson papers, Special Collections, Amherst College Library.

26   "For pity's sake don't": Longsworth, 133. On this same page of Longsworth there is an error, small, but which may as well be corrected since it touches on the question of the relations between Mabel Todd and Emily. Longsworth says that Mabel attended the funeral of Mrs. Dickinson in November 1882 "by request of Vinnie and Emily." But Mabel in her diary refers to "her daughter's request," meaning Vinnie. Emily is not mentioned.

27   Ned's complaint to his mother, and the difficulties that

ensued, are recorded by Mabel in her journal, Feb. 3, 1883 (194–195). See also Sewall, II, 175.

28   The almost daily socializing is recorded in Mabel's diary for January 1883. Besides entertaining Mattie or Austin at her own apartments, Mabel was at the Evergreens or in Sue's company on at least ten days in that three-week period.

28   "a long conversation": MLT journal, Feb. 3, 1883. Mabel's diary for January 8 includes this: "Mrs. Dickinson has just called; 11:30 A.M."

29   "Another slight misunderstanding": MLT journal, Feb. 3, 1883.

29   "exceedingly bright and entertaining": MLT diary, Feb. 4, 1883.

30   "He was a man who": Merriam, 216–217. Bowles's wife, it might be said in passing, was not unfailingly tolerant of these female friendships.

31   Mabel's sending flowers to Susan, and Sue's responding with a check, are in Longsworth, 160.

31   "It's too bad prudence": Leyda, II, 397; also in Longsworth, 160.

32   "Why should we censure": *Letters*, 889, which accepts Mrs. Todd's dating of "late 1885." The holograph at Amherst College has no date and neither salutation nor closing signature. For further details, see the next citation.

32   "Dear Sue—with the exception": *Letters*, 733, where it is dated by the editors as "about 1882," which certainly would include the following spring. That this note and the one cited next above are actually a pair, called forth by Emily's concern over the trouble next door, is a suggestion first made in my *Hidden Life of Emily Dickinson* (239–240, 272), and twenty years later I am more than ever of that opinion. Nothing since has arisen to dispute the attribution. From Emily herself comes proof that Austin did indeed talk to her of attending *Othello*: "Austin brought me the pickture of Salvini when he was last in Boston," she writes in fall 1884 (*Letters*, 847). Austin in his diary records seeing Tommaso Salvini as Othello in Boston in April 1883 (Leyda, II, 396).

33 "David ... writes that": MLT journal, Sept. 16, 1883 (204–205).

Chapter 2: *Mrs. Todd: Two Men for Me*

All fifteen extracts from Mabel Todd's journals in this chapter are quoted from the original at Yale, a single large-format manuscript volume of 282 numbered pages covering 1881–1885. The citations below supply page numbers in that volume. Dates of the entries are either clear in my text or are not needed.

36 "Everybody has been, as": journal, 141–146.

38 "I have been at Mrs. Dickinson's": journal, 149–157.

40 "He grows tremendously fonder": journal, 158–160. Mabel's wearing Ned's fraternity pin is described by herself in journal, 233.

41 "adultery ruined my life": Sewall, II, 293. He made the remark in 1933 to his daughter, Millicent, whose notes Sewall quotes.

41 "The dear boy felt more": journal, 161–163.

41 "walked in the woods": journal, 165.

42 "I am just now somewhat": journal, 170–171.

43 "This morning I had a long": diary, Sept. 6, 1882.

44 "Mr. Dickinson walked": diary, Sept. 8, 1882.

44 "Mr. Dickinson took": diary, Sept. 9, 1882.

45 The events of September 11, 1882, were later recalled by both Mabel and Austin: see Sewall, I, 176–177, and journal, 232.

45 "Everything is so joyous": journal, 172–178.

46 "Ned has been very devoted": journal, 185.

46 "I am not alone very": journal, 186–188.

47 "my chief joy": journal, 189.

47 "the most true and satisfying": journal, 191.

47 "David has had exceptional": journal, 193.

48 "I am not very happy just": journal, 194–196.

49 "David started this morning": journal, 197–198.

50 "went back to Winchester": journal, 203.

51 "At breakfast next morning": quoted from Longsworth, 165. Up to this point in her book Longsworth quotes from thirty-two letters and fragments that were exchanged clandestinely between Mabel and Austin, in which there is much open talk of love. None bears a date, and many of those written by Mabel are available only in copies later made by Austin. Most of these thirty-two excerpts do not fit the situation between the two this early, and they rather obviously belong to the period after December 1883, some long after, when the illicit affair actually began. Longsworth admits (127–129) the difficulties she had in establishing dates and a chronology for these and other letters, and that she was to an extent guided by Mabel Todd's own rough organization of them. I suggest that Mabel's dates for the letters in this early period are mostly spurious, meant to cloak the fact that her affair with Austin did not truly begin until after Gib's death. The letter quoted here, that of July 12, 1883, is the first of definite date and fits the circumstances. But this letter too has been tampered with (see the note for p. 119, below, p. 203).

51 "I remained in Washington": journal, 201–208.

55 "men of the world and": quoted in Sewall, I, 123. The phrase occurs in a letter of Austin's, of August 1893, a time when he was thinking of leaving Amherst and starting life afresh in Omaha.

Chapter 3: *My Ascended Playmate*

57 Emily's decision to withhold her work from publication, in my view, is directly related to its largely derivative nature—a fact for which there is abundant evidence, but which has not yet been sufficiently conceded. That fact in itself is important for its bearing on her later reversal of the decision. Where the marvelous technique (muted rhyme, daring diction, exploded grammar) is very much her own, the themes and the thought content of her poems have almost all been deftly borrowed, often in close

paraphrase, from other printed sources. This was her customary
procedure, her usual method of composition, doing deliberately
what so many other poets did occasionally and impulsively. Evidently lacking a facility for original observation, she borrowed
without stint, finding inspiration in "the little note that others
dropt" (poem No. 1009), and her art will never be properly
understood without an acknowledgment of this fact. To now,
such acknowledgment has been very grudging indeed. One recent critic, for example, in suggesting a larger significance for
Emily's undoubted borrowings actually, and soberly, dubs them
"moments of explicit allusiveness" (Diehl, *Romantic*, 8). A clever
phrase, and no doubt sincere, but not very helpful in getting at the
core of the poet's achievement since it rather deliberately obscures
a major element in her compositional procedure. Emily Dickinson studied the printed page as other poets study life, finding
there all the marvelous jumble of human nature handily brought
to focus. How well she used what she found is the real question for
critics to ponder. Susan Dickinson, for one, certainly knew of
Emily's borrowings, for there can be no other explanation of that
curious passage in the obituary she wrote that talks of Emily's
reading habits and concludes: "quick as the electric spark in her
intuitions and analyses, she seized the kernel instantly, almost
impatient of the fewest words by which she must make her
revelation" (see above, p. 112). Seizing the "kernel" of what she
read, then expressing it in stripped-down phrasing—"the fewest
words"—certainly describes nothing other than the writing of
derivative poetry, expressed in a *notably* compressed style. Anyone
so describing Emily's practice *must* have known the entire truth
about her composing methods. Sometime during, or just after,
the Civil War, as I have before suggested, Emily lost confidence,
deciding that poetry written in this fashion would be of little
worth, and so decided not to publish. She was wrong in that
conclusion, of course, for her achievement, putting aside its pro-
sodic limitations, is still of a very high order, her borrowings
undergoing a true sea change (of no poetry more than hers is the

rest of Shakespeare's phrase so appropriate: "rich and strange"). It needed twenty years, but I believe she finally came to realize the true value of what she had wrought, and it was this change of heart that opened her to the approach of Thomas Niles. An early discussion of the controverted topic of Emily's borrowings, particularly her undoubted large-scale use of Elizabeth Browning's *Aurora Leigh*, is in my previous book *The Hidden Life of Emily Dickinson*, 85–86, 89–109, 153–167. See also Capps, passim.

57   " 'H. H.' once told me": *Letters*, 726.

57   "The kind but incredible": *Letters*, 725. For further details of the Niles interlude, see *Letters*, 768–770.

60   On the possibility, or say likelihood, that Otis Lord, as well as being Emily's late love, was also her earlier "Master," recipient of the well-known letters, see my *Hidden Life*, 170–202. This ever-nagging question has apparently produced no consensus as yet, though Richard Sewall admits to finding the Lord thesis "tempting" (II, 644, and see 657, 658). Cynthia Wolff also agrees that there must have been *something* going on between Lord and Emily well before the death of Lord's wife in 1877 (see her *Emily Dickinson*, 385, 401, 406).

60   "Emily Jumbo! Sweetest": *Letters*, 747.

61   "You said with loved": *Letters*, 753.

61   For Otis Lord's visit to Amherst in fall 1883, a month before Gib's death, see Leyda, II, 404.

61   "I feel like wasting": *Letters*, 786. Same for the other quotation to Lord in this paragraph.

62   "There's sumthn else": *Letters*, 633. For "Cloudy Man," see *Letters*, 703. For "Mister Bridegroom," see *Letters*, 759.

62   "Memoirs of little boys": *Letters*, 673.

63   "My Dear Sally I thought": quoted from the original in Houghton Library; partially in Leyda, II, 389.

63   "with *his* little cane": Leyda, II, 397.

63   Gib's fall out of a carriage in August 1883 is recorded in a letter of his father's, quoted in Longsworth, 166. The boy was "dazed, and had some headache the next day." There was no

thought at the time of any link between this accident and the fatal illness three weeks later.

63   The progress of Gib's illness is reconstructed from documents in Leyda, II, 406, 412, 416; Sewall I, 205; *Letters*, 805; Bianchi, *Face*, 172–173; and Mabel Todd's diary, Oct. 5–6, 1883.

65   "Open the door, open": *Letters*, 803, also 891.

65   "My heart is breaking for": diary, Oct. 5, 1883.

66   "God help all you poor": quoted from the original in Houghton Library; partially in Leyda, II, 407.

66   "I can still hear him": Leyda, II, 407, quoting a letter of Samuel Bowles, Jr., no date given.

67   The obituary of Gib, unsigned, appeared in the *Amherst Record*, Oct. 17, 1883. There is no hint available as to its author. One item in it—recalling what I saw in the little room at the Evergreens—always stops me: the reference to Gib riding "his velocipede."

68   "I can but believe": *Letters*, 890. The remark is quoted by Emily in a letter of fall 1885, with the comment that it was the "only spar" they had in the terrible bereavement of two years before.

68   Emily's letters of sympathy to Susan after Gib's death are in *Letters*, 799–803.

70   "He seems entirely himself ": diary, Oct. 13, 1883.

71   "After Gilbert's death": Bianchi, *Face*, 174.

71   "revenge of the nerves": *Letters*, 827.

72   Medical prescriptions for Emily at this time, and for all the Dickinsons, were for long preserved by Adams' Drug Store of Amherst, and the originals are now at Amherst College. My initial study of them was made in 1969, when they were still in possession of the druggist, pasted into a thick volume.

72   "I shall make Wine Jelly": *Letters*, 814.

72   "After a brief unconsciousness": *Letters*, 816.

72   For Emily's physical collapse of June 1884, see her own description in *Letters*, 826. The October collapse was recorded in Austin's diary, quoted in Leyda, II, 433—she was found about 5:00 P.M.: "Since 3 o'clock alone—no one coming to help her—or

within call. Got her on to the lounge with Stephen's help and sent for Maggie."

73   "The little boy we laid away": *Letters*, 827.

Chapter 4: *Sword in the Family*

Mabel Todd's diary entries that are fully specified in the text are not repeated here. Except where otherwise stated the "journal" cited in this chapter is a *second* manuscript volume at Yale, this one covering the years 1885–1895.

74   "He says he should wish": journal (1881–1885), 213.

76   "staid a long time with": diary, Nov. 30, 1883.

76   That Mabel and Austin used the dining room at the Mansion to consummate their affair is stated in Longsworth, 173, though without citing specific evidence. Mabel's diary shows that she did go down to the Mansion that evening and even disguised the fact in her diary by giving the house a new name, The Pines, used only this once (the Mansion was surrounded by tall pine trees). In its entirety the entry for December 13 reads: "Painting in Walker Hall. Mrs. Emerson and Mrs. Hopkins came up to see me. Our friend came in to see me early [Austin]. In the afternoon I did various things at home, & David & I went out to see about some Christmas things. In the evening I went down to The Pines. A very happy evening. An Armenian came to the house just after dinner, with many Turkish goods. He is a student at the Agricultural College. I bought some lovely things." That Austin was at the Mansion that same evening is seen in his own diary for that day: "Bright, beautiful day. . . . Evg up at office, and at other house."

77   "All is tranquil": Austin to Mabel, Dec. 24, 1883, quoted in Longsworth, 175.

78   "My well beloved friend": journal (1881–1885), 219–220.

79   "Conventionalism is for": Longsworth, 186.

79   "[Austin's] life has been": journal, 8–9.

80   "I should like to go": journal, 10.

80   Mabel's hopes for Susan's early demise, of course in veiled language, are in the journal, 10, 22, 33, 34, 37, 46.

80   "daringly, defiantly": Longsworth, 192.

80   "Some men, I suppose": journal (1881–1885), 249–250.

81   "double life": Longsworth, 187.

82   "We are not to be frightened": Longsworth, 197.

82   "We will be more careful": Longsworth, 197.

83   "There is nothing to the": Longsworth, 199.

84   "witness" to sex: Longsworth, 242.

84   "reflects upon any other": Longsworth, 185.

85   "Why do you care to": Longsworth, 240.

85   "Fly in spider's Web": quoted from the original at Yale. See also Sewall, I, 190, where the list is characterized as "Austin's life as he described it to Mabel Todd." But that, as my text, I hope, shows, is going much too far.

85   "there is little to": Sewall, II, 190.

87   "it would cause him": Leyda, II, 19.

87   "Mother has read me her": Longsworth, 202. In an earlier letter (Jan. 26, 1885), to his sister, who had complained of upsets at college, Ned had written something similar: "There are worse things than disturbed sleep to be borne in this world—I can tell you—When you see one who is the Dearest thing in all the earth slowly being destroyed by cruelty—and no way in God's world to prevent it—and have to wear a smooth front all the time—then you know what it is to endure" (St. Armand, "Prodigal," 373). After studying some twenty of Ned's letters to his family of the mid-1880s (preserved at the Evergreens and not now available), St. Armand came to some forthright conclusions about the effect on Ned of his father's dallying. The letters show that Ned "gradually came to look upon his father with ill-suppressed anger and contempt," which eventually grew to "outright disdain, if not actual hatred" (372, 375). This is very probable, but in passing it might be said that the actual quotations supplied do not quite support so violent a reaction.

88   "a woman who has brought": Ned to Vinnie, Aug. 27, 1896, quoted from my *Hidden Life*, 242.

88   "to roam in my": *Letters*, 903.

88   Mabel's visits to the Mansion 1882–1886 have been calculated from her diaries.

90   Emily's letters to Mabel: by now it should be clear that despite Mabel's later claims to have received a veritable stream of letters from Emily, on only two occasions did Emily actually write her. The first was to thank her for the Indian pipe painting (Nos. 769–770), the second sent at Austin's request when Mabel was in Europe (No. 1004). Two or three other scraps of writing accompanied flowers.

91   "that she might know of ": Longsworth, 208. A few days later Austin wrote Mabel again, saying, "I see Vin and Em more than I did—and you are the constant theme," and shortly after that he wrote, "I have two or three visits with my sisters everyday and we talk you over always" (Longsworth, 216, 226). None of these mentions, of course, proves anything about Emily's feelings toward Mabel, only that she was willing to listen to her brother talk. Nor can it even be guessed as to what Austin may have said at these sessions. Very likely it was all simply general appreciation of Mabel's well-advertised charm and talent.

91   "I love you, and I": Longsworth, 204–205.

92   Austin's bringing Mabel the news of Emily's May 13 collapse is in her diary for that day: "My friend about noon. Emily sick. I went over there after dinner. No change. . . . Mr. Dickinson in the evening." The other facts in this paragraph are from Mabel's diary for May 14–15. Also see Leyda, II, 470–471.

92   "would not wake again": Austin's diary, May 15.

Chapter 5: *Called Back?*

94   The brief remission of Emily's illness in spring 1886 is in *Letters*, 903: "I have been very ill, Dear Friend, since November, bereft of Book and Thought, by the doctor's reproof, but begin to roam in my room now."

94   "Little Cousins, Called": *Letters*, 906. This brief, undated note is taken to be Emily's last, and is so positioned in *Letters*. In

any case, it was certainly written after January 1885, when Emily mentioned in another note her reading of Hugh Conway's novel *Called Back*. Even if the little note were not her actual last, it could still perform the function I suggest. A pertinent question is this: if the words do not have the meaning usually assigned, then *what* do they mean?

94 "She would walk by": Leyda, II, 471.

94 "stark, unconscious": Austin's diary, in Leyda, II, 470.

95 "looked 30, not a gray": Leyda, II, 475.

96 "the wealth of auburn": Leyda, II, 476.

96 Emily's funeral: Bianchi, *Life*, 101–102; Bianchi, *Face*, 61–62; Leyda, II, 474–475. The bier, made by the funeral director, is listed in his bill (Jones Library) at $2.50.

97 ED poems that reflect a suicidal mood, in order:

Quoted phrase	*Variorum No.*	*First line*
"cordial grave"	1625	Back from the cordial
"So give me back"	1632	So give me back
"to that aetherial"	1596	Few, yet enough
"The spirit looks"	1630	As from the earth
"denied the privilege"	1597	'Tis not the swaying
"*rumored* springs"	1606	Quite empty, quite
"Each that we lose"	1605	Each that we lose
"beckons spaciously"	1626	No life can pompless
"Is there no wandering"	1631	Oh Future! thou

In addition, there are a number of other poems of these late years that brood heavily on the question of death, though without an overt link to suicide: 1603, 1604, 1609, 1610, 1613, 1620, 1633, 1634. A proper and inescapable question, of course, is whether all these poems, or any of them, have a close personal application to ED's life at this time. But any discussion of the point must begin with the *fact* that she wrote in this period so many verses dealing so openly with suicide and death.

97 Suicide as an ED theme: This has been very little treated or noted in Dickinson studies. The most extended previous

efforts occur in David Porter, *Dickinson: The Modern Idiom*, 286–290, and John Cody, *After Great Pain*, 251–252, 296–298. Porter concludes that suicide for Emily was "not an actual possibility," though he notes that "the subject lured even as it baffled." But his evidence is incomplete, since for some reason not clear he has ignored the later suicide and death poems listed here. Cody, on the other hand, finds that Emily had definite "suicidal inclinations," though offering no specific evidence. He even suggests, as his reading of poem No. 1692, that she may have "once actually attempted suicide." His discussion, however, concentrates on ED's middle years. Poem No. 1692, which exists only in a transcript made by Sue, is undatable. Also, its eight rather bland lines somehow seem less personal than the other suicide poems quoted in this chapter.

100 "a loved paragraph which": *Letters*, 902. In the same letter she mentions a current murder sensation, the poisoning death of a local woman.

101 "We buried him, to the": *Wuthering Heights*, Chap. 34, para. 32. Some of Heathcliff's tormented soliloquies toward the end might have been spoken by Emily herself as she yearned for reunion with the dead Judge Lord: "I cannot continue in this condition! I have to remind myself to breathe—almost to remind my heart to beat! I have a single wish, and my whole being and faculties are yearning to attain it. They have yearned toward it so long, and so unwaveringly, that I'm convinced it *will* be reached. . . . O God! it is a long fight, I wish it were over!"

102 Quotations from Austin's diaries are made from the originals at Yale. See also Leyda, II, 471.

Chapter 6: *Vinnie Takes a Hand*

All references to Mabel Todd's journal in this chapter are to the manuscript volume for 1885–1895.

104 "inspired devotion": Sewall, II, 22. Same for the three other comments in this paragraph, 216, 219, 151.

105 "devoted labor": Wolff, 6.

105 "actually trembling with": *Harper's Magazine* CLX (1930). Same for the other quotations in this paragraph.

106 "detachment and objectivity": Bingham, *Brocades*, 348.

107 "willing to play friendly": Longsworth, 259.

108 "They seemed to open": journal, 73, entry dated Nov. 30, 1890. Also in Bingham, *Brocades*, 402.

108 Mabel's quotation of the Lucy Larcom sonnet is in her journal for Feb. 22, 1890, 54.

109 "The extent of her writing": manuscript note by Austin, original at Yale. It was used by Mabel in preparing her Preface for Emily's second volume.

109 "a Joan of Arc feeling": Bingham, *Brocades,* 87.

112 Higginson's wanting to use the obituary as preface for Emily's first volume is in his letter, Bingham, *Brocades*, 61–62, where it is claimed that Vinnie did the refusing. But Mabel had earlier claimed that it was Susan herself who refused permission (Taggard, 331). Of course, this was an outright lie, for Sue learned of the book only as it appeared: in mid-December 1890 she wrote Higginson that she was "dazed by the announcement of Emily's poems in the Xtian Union. . . . It was my first intimation that strange hands were preparing them for publication" (Bingham, *Brocades*, 86). She soon rallied, however, and expressed her decided pleasure in the book: "I delight in such recognition of her genius as I have known and felt it since our early girl-hood intimacy" (Bingham, *Brocades*, 114).

113 Higginson's visit to the Evergreens on Sept. 29, 1886, is in his diary: "To Amherst. Staid at Austin Dickinson's—beautiful drive with him round Amherst" (from the original at Boston Public Library). The entry for the thirtieth—"Ret. fr. Amherst"— shows he was in town, and thus at the Evergreens, overnight.

113 "unpresentable": quoted in a letter of Susan to Higginson, Bingham, *Brocades*, 86. Same for the other quotation in this paragraph.

114 "dreading publicity for": Bingham, *Brocades*, 115.

115 "quaint bits to my": Bingham, *Brocades*, 86. Same for the other quotation in this paragraph.

115 "my disappointed endeavors": Bingham, *Brocades*, 87.

115 "expecting to become famous": Bingham, *Brocades*, 66.

116 "Philol. Com.": Higginson's diary, July 11, 1888, quoted from the original. The full entry reads: "At Amherst. Philol Com. & drove with Martha Dickinson to Bp. Huntington's fine old farm in No. Hadley. Home in after." The entry for the tenth reads: "After. to Amherst. Staid at Austin Dickinson's." The inside back cover of the diary contains a handwritten list of Higginson's many clubs and societies.

116 "After my brief talk": Bingham, *Brocades*, 87.

117 "I feel as if I had": Longsworth, 305.

117 "unlimited drives": journal, 33.

118 "Keep cool and own": Longsworth, 309.

118 "I have been very": Longsworth, 310–312.

119 "I suffer for every wound": Sewall, I, 179, where it is given as part of a letter of July 12, 1883 (the whole letter may be read in Longsworth, 164–166). But examination of the original at Yale shows that these words are on a separate piece of paper, carefully torn, which does not belong to the main letter (the folds and the lining do not match). Also, the contents of this separate paragraph, and its tone, do not fit the circumstances before the affair began in earnest after Gib's death that October. The summer of 1888, as my text indicates, seems the likely place for it.

120 "she begged me to copy": journal, 71.

121 "Get that woman's name": manuscript autobiography of Martha Dickinson, unpublished, seen at the Evergreens in 1985.

121 "The outlook was appalling": journal, 71.

121 "Frequently [Vinnie] came": Bingham, *Brocades*, 31.

123 "In the afternoon I went": diary, Nov. 6, 1889. For the general facts of this Boston contact between Mabel and Higginson, see Longsworth, 321, 326–327.

123 "Col. Higginson called": journal, 75–76.

124 "worked hard for twelve": Longsworth, 327.

126 "I daresay you are aware": Bingham, *Brocades*, 60.

126 "Nothing is going to": Bingham, *Brocades*, 61. It is unlikely that Mabel responded, or responded truthfully, to Higgin-

son's request for help in deciphering Vinnie's letter. If he knew Vinnie was against listing Mabel as coeditor, he certainly would not have so airily dismissed her request.

127   "Scornful disregard": quoted in Bingham, *Brocades*, 74.

127   "I feel as if we": quoted in Bingham, *Brocades*, 81.

127   "the book is out, and": journal, 81–82. The whole entry occupies pages 68–85, while the portion dealing with publication of the poems is on 70–82. It is printed in Bingham, *Brocades*, 401–405.

128   Austin's thought of heading west is in his letter of Aug. 8, 1893, to a business acquaintance in Omaha, Sewall, I, 123. His four suicidal remarks are in Longsworth, 343, 347, 349.

129   "there was a tilt, however": Bianchi, *Face*, 134.

130   "small, narrow-minded": journal, 36.

Chapter 7: *Lawsuit: The Final Puzzle*

The primary sources for this treatment of the Todd-Dickinson trial are three legal documents preserved in the Todd papers at Yale. Of first importance is a lengthy (fifty-one oversize pages) printed transcript of the trial evidence, prepared for use in the Todds' unsuccessful appeal of the decision: *Supreme Judicial Court, Hampshire County, September Law Sitting 1898, Defendant's Appeal* (cited below as *Appeal*). There is also a *Plaintiff's Brief* (thirteen pages) and a *Defendant's Brief* (eleven pages), containing the attorneys' written arguments in the appeal. These documents were also used in Longsworth, 409–422, but Longsworth gives only three brief, less than significant extracts, while allowing equal time to a long, self-serving passage from Mabel's journal. Earlier Mrs. Bingham used them in discussing the trial (*Brocades*, 349–367), but in her usual desultory fashion. Newspaper reports of the trial appeared in the *Springfield Republican*, March 1, 2, 4, and April 16.

131   "were estranged": *Appeal*, 43. Same for the other two quotations in this paragraph.

133   "Mabel Loomis Todd did": *Appeal*, 1–2. Same for the quotations in the preceding and following paragraphs.

135 Mrs. Bingham's reference to *opéra bouffe* is in *Brocades*, 359. The remark is based on the memories of a friend, Mary Jordan, who had attended the trial and who described Vinnie's behavior in her replies on the witness stand as rather like a clown, a charge contradicted by the clear evidence of the transcript.

135 "Mrs. Todd asked me": *Appeal*, 17.

136 "Early in the winter": *Appeal*, 17.

136 "[Please tell us] whether": *Appeal*, 17–19.

138 "I never had in mind": *Appeal*, 19.

139 "Mrs. Todd asked the privilege": *Appeal*, 20.

139 "I never stated to [Mr. Hills]": *Appeal*, 21. Recalled to the stand the second day, Vinnie quoted Dwight Hills as saying of the Todds, "They are leeches, leeches, leeches" (*Appeal*, 50). The remark was reported in the *Springfield Republican* next day, March 4, as Vinnie knew it would be.

140 "I opened the door myself": *Appeal*, 22–23.

141 The real estate estimated value for the property was provided by Dwight Palmer, one of the executors of Austin's estate, who aided Vinnie's lawyers in the case, *Appeal*, 24.

141 "Austin Dickinson, a": *Appeal*, 10–11.

142 "In early September, 1895": *Appeal*, 25–26.

143 "I asked Miss Dickinson": *Appeal*, 26–28.

144 "I never said anything to": *Appeal*, 30–31.

145 "The only object of your": *Appeal*, 34–36.

148 "I told him not to record": *Appeal*, 36.

148 "I saw her first on that": *Appeal*, 37–39.

149 "I bought this building lot": *Appeal*, 39.

150 "I never in the evening or": *Appeal*, 49–50.

151 "I was just going out": *Appeal*, 50.

151 "Miss Dickinson herself": *Appeal*, 40–43.

153 "The earlier part of the": *Appeal*, 42.

153 "Have you said in conversation": *Appeal*, 43.

154 "Mrs. Todd gave a reason": *Appeal*, 43–44.

155 "She spoke to me first on": *Appeal*, 48–49.

156 "It was in Mr. Hills' room": *Appeal*, 46.

156 "never said anything": *Appeal*, 46.

156 "no material testimony": *Appeal*, 51. For the deposition of Maggie Maher, and the surrounding circumstances, see Longsworth, 412–413. That Maggie did in fact say something on the stand that was unwelcome to the Todds seems to be referred to in the news reports: She was "called to testify in behalf of the plaintiff as to conversation that had taken place between Mrs. Todd and Miss Dickinson but it was ruled out on objection of the defendant" (*Hampshire Gazette*, March 3, 1898). Perhaps the voluble servant blurted out something not asked for by the question, though it is not clear from this report whether it was the question itself that was ruled out, or the answer.

157 "refinement and seclusion": *Plaintiff's Brief*, 5. Same for the other quotations in this paragraph. Summations are not included in the printed *Appeal* but became a part of both sides' accompanying briefs.

158 "that a long-time professor": *Defendant's Brief*, 11.

158 "It is ordered, adjudged": *Appeal*, 14. Concerning Spaulding's evidence, the *Springfield Republican*, March 4, stated that it "was not so conclusive as many had anticipated it would be." The same paper in announcing the decision on April 16 said the outcome "was foretold several weeks ago."

159 "did not consider it of ": *Appeal*, 21. This was said by Vinnie on the witness stand (see above, p. 140).

160 "attend to it and get the": *Appeal*, 49.

160 "with the request that she": Bingham, *Brocades*, 338. This use of Austin's note in *Brocades* is misleading. Undated, the note is given in a vague context of the 1890s, making its promise seem to be compensation for Mabel's work on the poems. But Austin's will was actually made on Nov. 3, 1887 (copy at Yale), long before Mabel began her copying, a fact of which Mrs. Bingham was certainly aware.

160 "I find she is going": diary, Oct. 6, 1895.

161 "I send you today by": Bingham, *Brocades*, 334.

161 "I am glad to hear that": Bingham, *Brocades*, 334.

161 Mabel's reception of the proofs for *Poems, Third Series*, is noted in Bingham, *Brocades*, 339, as is her trip to Boston in

January 1896, as well as her reference to writing the Preface. Of course, in *Brocades* the three items simply happened to come together and are not given the interpretation suggested in my text.

162   Vinnie's motivation: aside from her care for her sister's poems, I am inclined to think that Vinnie had another reason for acting as she did in bringing suit against Mabel. Only recently, I believe, had she become fully convinced of the adulterous connection of her brother with the married Mrs. Todd, not previously being able to credit any rumors she may have heard, particularly in the presence of Mabel's husband. The thing that convinced her, I suggest, was a packet of Mabel's letters to Austin, left with Vinnie to be burned unopened in case of Austin's death (Sewall, I, 178). The letters were not burned. Also, and especially because Austin's legacy was the point of the contention, I believe that Susan herself somehow had a hand in what happened—but here the matter runs off into speculation, legitimate enough, but lacking all documentation. For some discussion see Bingham, *Brocades*, the Longsworth volume, and my own *Hidden Life*.

Chapter 8: *Mabel's Victory*

163   "She was a woman of": *Amherst Record*, May 14, 1913. The *Republican* obituary was of the same date.

164   "Poor old Susan died last night": diary, May 13, 1913, quoted from Sewall, I, 194, where it appears along with this gratuitous comment by Sewall: "At least she seems to have understood, as Emily did, the paradox and power of Sue's nature." Here is final proof, if it were needed, of where the biographer's sympathies lay.

164   "freer in my mind and": a Mabel Todd autobiographical fragment, written about 1930, quoted in Sewall, I, 291. Same for the other quotations in this paragraph.

166   Josephine Pollitt's approach to Mrs. Todd, according to a note by Mabel in the Todd papers at Yale, was made as early as 1924, when the young woman was preparing a dissertation on ED

at Columbia University. Genevieve Taggard's link with Mrs. Todd also began well before 1930 (see her correspondence in the Todd papers at Yale, some excerpts from which are quoted in Sewall, I, 253). Both women credit Mabel in their acknowledgments.

166   "Sue proved to be a blind": Taggard, 130–131.

167   "Mrs. Todd apprehended": Pollitt, 309–310.

167   "Mrs. Todd was one of ": Taggard, 375–376. If these early biographers, as well as later ones, had consulted the record of the Todd-Dickinson trial of 1898, they would have found Mabel replying on the witness stand to a direct question under oath: "I never saw Miss Emily Dickinson except as I saw her flitting through a dark hall. She had spoken to me. I never spoke to her" (*Appeal*, 29). That admission went unnoticed, and it was not until 1971 that anyone thought to question Mabel's "intimacy" with the poet (see Walsh, 41).

168   "It should be clearly stated": Whicher, 311. He also came near ignoring Martha's two books about her aunt (1924, 1932), consulting them only for the texts of some of Emily's letters and for information "about the family library and about the reading of Austin, Susan, and Lavinia" (328). Biographers since Whicher have tended to follow his example, making much of Martha's admitted errors of detail, while ignoring her valuable views of the living Emily she knew so well.

168   "brought into the closely": Whicher, 33–35. The three "proofs" are on p. 35. Whicher does not in his book cite any source for his view of Susan's character, though he fully discusses the background for each individual chapter. Neither does he in his acknowledgments mention getting help from Mabel Todd. But that he actually did so is disclosed by a passing reference to his having consulted "many unpublished letters" written by Mabel, Higginson, Austin, and Vinnie. "These documents," he explains, "have since passed into the possession of Mrs. Walter V. Bingham of New York" (328). The word "since" in that passage shows that he read these letters before they passed to Mabel's daughter, Mrs. Bingham, and thus while they were still in Mabel's own hands.

170   "Facts no longer need be": Bingham, *Brocades*, ix.

170   "Susan's daughter was still": Bingham, *Brocades*, viii.

171   "From the few allusions": Bingham, *Brocades*, 218–219.

172   "I have failed to find": Letter to Mrs. Bingham from Lucy Kellog, Aug. 4, 1930, as quoted in Sewall, I, 282 (an appendix). Despite his having this letter available, Sewall in his main text (102) while discussing Susan's background quotes the phrase from *Brocades* about her father's "convivial habits," then adds, "There is no clear indication that the girls suffered any embarrassment in the town from their origins." How much better to have mentioned the researcher's exonerating letter at this point in the text, rather than relegate it to a parenthetical insert in an unrelated appendix. This casual defamation of the unfortunate Thomas Gilbert is continued in Longsworth, 69–71.

172   Mary Lee Hall: the facts on her background have been kindly supplied by Daniel Lombardo, Jones Library, Amherst. She was born in New York City in 1865, and while in Amherst lived with her parents on Gray Street. It is obvious from her letters that she never really understood why Susan should have been so "jealous" of Mabel Todd, or angry with Vinnie ("Vinnie knew too much about her," she thought [Sewall, I, 230]). By the time Miss Hall became friendly with Vinnie, the Austin-Mabel-Sue matter had long been settled in its final pattern and certainly was not a subject of conversation with an outsider. Enough comment, perhaps, is the fact that Miss Hall later claimed to have continued as good friends with *both* Mabel and Vinnie after the lawsuit.

172   "after Ned's death": Bingham, *Brocades*, 371.

172   "Vinnie was not well all": Bingham, *Brocades*, 372–373.

173   "[Vinnie] told me Sue": Bingham, *Brocades*, 374.

174   "domestic tribulation": Bingham, *Home*, 55, which also talks knowingly of "Austin's early disappointment in his marriage." The context here is Mrs. Bingham's claim that all references to Susan were deleted from Emily's published letters in 1894 at the specific demand of Austin—of course, an operation more likely to have been Mabel's own doing (*Home*, 411).

174 "Nor had Austin foreseen": Bingham, *Home*, 409. In the same year that *Home* was published, Mrs. Bingham also brought out *Emily Dickinson: A Revelation*, containing the love letters to Otis Lord. Even in this slim volume, where there was no need to mention Sue more than in passing, she receives a paragraph of condemnation. Emily "squandered her affections" on Sue, and soon the poet "withered in the atmosphere of disharmony that was not slow to develop in the house next door," etc. (*Revelation*, 7). Mrs. Bingham may have had something further in mind, for in the Todd papers at Yale (Series VII, Box 102), there is a type-written manuscript by her which tries to show by an interpreta-tion of Austin's diaries that there was an almost total lack of rapport between him and his family (Gilbert excepted). The quo-tations from the diary are highly selective, and for anyone familiar with all the documents and the background in general the distor-tion is obvious. In her various writings Mrs. Bingham appears to have made no direct use of this document, but something quite similar may be seen in Sewall, I, 190–191. The diary entries mentioned by Sewall concern several parties that were held at the Evergreens, to all of which Austin objected. Two of the parties were given for the epileptic Ned, and one of these, held to cele-brate his twenty-first birthday, was styled by Austin a "wild tear and revel." Quoting briefly from five entries, Sewall concludes sweepingly that the diary shows Austin's interests to have "dif-fered diametrically from those of his wife." Another reader might judge from the same entries that Austin could be downright crabby when his routine was upset.

175 "She had a grief of origin": Higgins, 37–38. The only voice to speak in defense of Sue during this long period, so far as I can find, was my own in *Hidden Life*, 240–241. The first extended effort on Sue's behalf did not come until 1983, when an article, "In Defense of Sue," by Dorothy Oberhaus appeared in *Dickinson Studies* No. 43, 1–25. Earnest and well reasoned, the article makes use of the original materials published by Sewall, and analyzes Emily's letters and poems to Sue, finally showing that Mabel and

her daughter must be set down as "prejudiced and unreliable" witnesses. Surprising is the fact that no mention of this article appears in Longsworth's *Austin and Mabel* or in any other Dickinson study published since. Even the descriptions of it in the two most recent Dickinson bibliographies (Dandurand and Boswell) are quite inadequate, neither making clear that Oberhaus succeeds in raising legitimate doubts about the integrity of Mabel and her daughter. An earlier, more tentative defense of Susan in her relations with the poet was that by Jean Mudge (*Prairie Schooner*, 1978), which demonstrates that Susan was of great importance to Emily, both personally and artistically, through most of her life. Mudge concludes: "At no time does there appear a radical break or turning away from each other. . . . Emily's notes document regular and happy rendezvous with Sue in the Mansion until 1883" (104). But Mudge's article, too, has been ignored. For another effort to demonstrate Susan's importance to Emily, especially as a poet, see Morris, "Two Sisters Have I," *Massachusetts Review* (1981).

175 "Ten years later she gave": Sewall, I, xii. Same for the other quotations in this paragraph.

176 "ultimate clarity may": Sewall, I, 12.

177 "signs of trouble ahead": Sewall, I, 103. Sewall's analysis of Austin's courtship letters is in I, 103–113. The five extracts occur on pp. 107, 108, 109, 111, 113. Thereafter casual references to Austin's "private sorrow" (120), "domestic misery" (145), and "wretched domestic life" (187) are frequent.

177 "What Edward failed to": Sewall, I, 162.

178 "In the light of what": Sewall, I, 103.

178 "Sue's temperament, tastes": Sewall, I, 115.

179 "But for Austin not only": Sewall, I, 116.

179 "He once remarked to Mrs.": Sewall, I, 117.

180 "The ill feeling between the": Sewall, I, 161.

180 "mainly from Mabel Todd's": Sewall, I, 171.

180 "She was every inch a": Sewall, I, 171.

181 "the rhetoric soars to": Sewall, I, 181. Same for the three

other quotations in this paragraph, 183, 184. Not every reader, it should be said, will be able to detect many of those awesome crescendos in Austin's frequently gaseous epistolary style.

181   The "spasmodic" passage reads in its entirety:

> Thus the Todds were well launched, to the delight of all. The relations between the two families ran smoothly for at least the first year and a half. But this pleasant state of affairs did not last. Mabel soon learned that Susan Dickinson was known in town for her violent but short-lived enthusiasms. She took people up—and dropped them capriciously, a fate (Mabel was warned) that might befall even Sue's 'darling Toddy.' Sue, however, was not the immediate cause of trouble. What led to an open break was that Ned, Austin and Sue's twenty-year-old son, in his enthusiasm over this brilliant newcomer, fell in love with her, all within the first few months of the Todds' arrival. (Sewall, I, 174).

A strange sentence, that one: "Sue, however, was not the immediate cause of trouble." Sue was not the cause of trouble *at all*, so why mention her as a possible source of the trouble? What led to the "open break" was not Ned's falling for the newcomer, it was the newcomer's sneaking flirtation with both father and son.

182   Mrs. Todd's autobiographical manuscripts at Yale: There are three, all typewritten, which have been combined and printed in Sewall, I, 275–292. The steady stream of Mabel's deliberate lies and half-truths in this document will be apparent to anyone who has read with care through the present work. Inevitably, of course, Sewall's amalgamation has become a convenient biographical quarry for "facts" about Mabel, Sue, Emily, Vinnie, and the publication of the poems.

182   "Mary Lee Hall's bias": Sewall, I, 252.

183   "evil-minded . . . a fiend": Sewall, I, 261.

183   "the local gossip about": Sewall, I, 231.

183   "questionable relationship": Sewall, II, 471. The phrase occurs in some notes made by Mrs. Bingham of a 1934 conversation with Mary Jordan, then aged about eighty and no friend of Sue. Further excerpts are given in a Sewall appendix

(I, 262–264), containing such casually vicious remarks as "Sue a woman who despised her husband and was the soul mate of Sam Bowles."

183 "the materials to go on": Sewall, I, 197.

183 "there is no clear evidence": Sewall, I, 198.

184 Mrs. Jameson's remark occurs in a letter to her son. Sewall's three (graduated) references to it are in I, 198, 204, 214. The pertinent phrase in the letter reads: "Miss Emily Dickinson . . . went over to Austin's with Maggie the night Gilbert died, the first time she had been in the house for 15 years" (Leyda, II, 406). The Jamesons were neighbors but not close friends of either Dickinson family, so just why the woman's offhand remark should be accepted as the final word on Emily's relations with the Evergreens is a puzzle (Sewall is not the only one to have used it). Usually, scholarship requires a good deal more evidence than that for so sweeping a conclusion. The excesses such professional lapses can generate are to be seen in much of the recent literature. For instance, there is this remark about Emily and Sue in a 1985 lecture given at the Pierpont Morgan Library under sponsorship of the Academy of American Poets: "A serious rift occurred between the two women beginning about 1868 so that personal visits ceased for fifteen years. Austin's wife became socially ambitious, haughty and dominating. . . . Sue's mercurial temper, even cruelty, was felt early by Emily" (Swenson, 34). Simply by subtracting the mythical fifteen years from 1883, the lecturer has been able to posit what no one ever claimed, that there grew a "serious rift" between the friends as early as 1868—a time when, as all the evidence shows, Emily was closest to Sue and to her young son and infant daughter.

185 "One further thought suggests": Sewall, I, 150.

186 "Beautiful as the letter": Sewall, I, 205.

186 "Sue hovered dominant": Longsworth, 68. Along the same lines is the following typical bit of novelizing (69), a veritable soap opera touch (harsh words but true), which recurs throughout the book. In Austin's youthful courtship letters, writes Longsworth:

Sue stands congealed at the center of a morass of feeling that Austin confesses to indulging for the first time. Unable to lead him through his emotional mire as he somehow expected she would, equally unable to make a move on her own behalf without setting Austin's bog quaking and trembling, Sue was effectively trapped in Austin's vision of her—a highly uncooperative soul figure, the bright aspect of his innermost strivings, an investiture inevitably destined to disappoint cruelly.

Who would have thought that so much of penetrating insight into the souls of two long-dead people could be extracted so confidently from the scribbled drafts of old letters! Shakespeare's sonnets yield hardly more about that other Dark Lady.

187   "they became accessory": Longsworth, 5.

187   "incredible": Longsworth, xi.

187   "It isn't hard to understand": Longsworth, 116.

187   "conflicted personality": Longsworth, 67. Same for the other two quotations in this paragraph.

187   "the rich lode of ": Longsworth, 443.

187   "faith and enthusiasm": Longsworth, 434. An instance of Sewall's enthusiasm occurs in the Preface he contributed to the Longsworth volume: "According to the letters, every moment apart was a strain. Those letters! Long, passionate, well composed, and sometimes beautiful. 'The awesome fervor of their love': I am more than ever convinced of it. They called it overwhelming, God-inspired, beyond any love that ever was. . . ." A few lines further down he refers to this "drama of two sensitive people," obscuring the fact that one of these sensitive people spent most of her nights in another man's bed. This same obscuration of a third actor in the seedy drama continues through much of Longsworth's treatment of the affair. And in truth neither Sewall nor Longsworth seems to have dwelt overmuch on the possibility that Susan and her children might also be considered sensitive people.

Another aspect of the Longsworth book must be noted, especially in view of her claims to documentary precision (and Sewall's similar claim in his Preface to Longsworth): the book contains *no* documentation, *no* notes or references beyond a general bibliography of published works and a list of collections consulted at various libraries. For the thousands of facts woven together to form the narrative, derived from a wide range of documents, there are no individual citations whatever. A reader wishing to analyze arguments or conclusions, or test quotations and chronology, is faced with an endless task in his search for specific sources. For anyone unfamiliar with the original documents, it would be impossible.

188   A recent (1986) massive and much-admired critical biography of Emily Dickinson, that by Cynthia Wolff, will serve as an illustration of how the Todd impostures regarding Sue have enmeshed themselves in contemporary Dickinson scholarship. Never stopping to question her sources, Wolff in discussing the reality behind the poetry makes blithely assured use of the following: the "troubled" courtship of Sue and Austin (5, 115, 571), Sue's "flawed" character and personality (5, 429, 571), the "strained" marriage (5, 176, 492, 536), Sue's "fear" of sex and pregnancy (396, 553, 573), Sue's "flirtation" and worse with Sam Bowles (250, 391–392, 398), the "break" between Sue and Emily (492, 529). Unaccountably, Wolff adds another item to the long list of Sue's failings, of course omitting proofs. The complaint this time is on the score of religious faith, an area of Sue's life not before invaded. In full certainty, Wolff states: "The early fervor of her faith dwindled into a comfortable acceptance of polite, Sunday-go-to-church religion" (429). Probably that will be the last. By now there isn't enough left intact of Sue's good name and character to make further condemnation worth the trouble.

Selected Bibliography

Listed here are those sources, published and unpublished, which are cited in the text or notes or which have provided specific background information. Also included are several items which have afforded a more general stimulus during the course of research and study.

Banning, Evelyn. *Helen Hunt Jackson*. New York: Vanguard, 1973.

Barker, Wendy. *Lunacy of Light, Emily Dickinson and the Experience of Metaphor*. Carbondale, Ill.: Southern Illinois University Press, 1987.

Bianchi, Martha. *Emily Dickinson Face to Face*. Boston: Houghton Mifflin, 1932.

_____. *Life and Letters of Emily Dickinson*. Boston: Houghton Mifflin, 1924.

Bingham, Millicent. *Ancestors' Brocades: The Literary Debut of Emily Dickinson*. New York: Harper, 1945.

_____. *Emily Dickinson: A Revelation*. New York: Harper, 1954.

_____. *Emily Dickinson's Home: Letters of Edward Dickinson and His Family*. New York: Harper, 1955.

Blackmur, Richard. "Emily Dickinson: Notes on Prejudice and Fact." *Southern Review* (Fall 1937), 323–347.

Boswell, Jeanetta. *Emily Dickinson: A Bibliography 1890–1987*. Jefferson, N.C.: McFarland & Co., 1990.

Bowles, Samuel. Letters of, to Susan and Austin Dickinson, 1858–1878. Dickinson papers, Houghton Library, Harvard.

Burgess, John. *Reminiscences of an American Scholar*. New York: Columbia University Press, 1934.

Capps, Jack. *Emily Dickinson's Reading*. Cambridge, Mass.: Harvard University Press, 1966.

Chase, Richard. *Emily Dickinson*. New York: Sloane Assoc., 1951.

Cody, John. *After Great Pain: The Inner Life of Emily Dickinson*. Cambridge, Mass.: Harvard University Press, 1971.

Dandurand, Karen. *Dickinson Scholarship, an Annotated Bibliography*, 1969–1985. New York: Garland, 1988.

———. "New Dickinson Civil War Publications." *American Literature* (March 1984), 17–27.

Dickinson, Susan. "Annals of the Evergreens." Typewritten manuscript of twenty-six pages, dated July 1892. Dickinson papers, Houghton Library, Harvard. Edited version in *Amherst College Alumni Magazine* (Spring 1981).

———. "Society at Amherst Half a Century Ago." Typewritten manuscript of twenty-five pages, undated but about 1895. Dickinson papers, Houghton Library, Harvard. Edited version in *Essays on Amherst History*. Amherst, Mass.: Vista Press, 1978.

Diehl, Joanne. *Dickinson and the Romantic Imagination*. Princeton: Princeton University Press, 1988.

Eberwein, Jane. *Emily Dickinson: Strategies of Limitation*. Amherst: University of Massachusetts Press, 1985.

Erskine, John. "The Dickinson Feud." In *The Memory of Certain Persons*. New York: Lippincott, 1947.

Ferlazzo, Paul. *Emily Dickinson*. Boston: Twayne, 1976.

Franklin, Ralph. *The Editing of Emily Dickinson*. Madison: Wisconsin University Press, 1967.

Frothingham, Theodore. Letters of, to Susan Dickinson. Dickinson papers, Houghton Library, Harvard. Same for letters of Susan Dickinson to Theodore Frothingham.

Griffith, Clark. *The Long Shadow: Emily Dickinson's Tragic Poetry*. Princeton: Princeton University Press, 1964.

Higgins, David. *Portrait of Emily Dickinson: The Poet and Her Prose.* New Brunswick, N.J.: Rutgers University Press, 1967.

Johnson, Thomas, ed. *The Poems of Emily Dickinson.* Cambridge, Mass.: The Belknap Press of Harvard University Press, 1955 (variorum edition). 3 vols.

_____. *The Letters of Emily Dickinson.* Cambridge, Mass.: The Belknap Press of Harvard University Press, 1958. 3 vols.

Keller, Karl. *The Only Kangaroo Among the Beauty: Emily Dickinson and America.* Baltimore: Johns Hopkins University Press, 1979.

Kher, Inder. *The Landscape of Absence: Emily Dickinson's Poetry.* New Haven: Yale University Press, 1974.

Leyda, Jay. *The Years and Hours of Emily Dickinson.* New Haven: Yale University Press, 1960. 2 vols.

Longsworth, Polly. *Austin and Mabel: The Amherst Affair and Love Letters of Austin Dickinson and Mabel Loomis Todd.* New York: Farrar, Straus and Giroux, 1984.

McNeil, Helen. *Emily Dickinson.* New York: Pantheon, 1986.

Merriam, George. *Life and Times of Samuel Bowles.* New York: Century Co., 1885.

Monteiro, George. "Love and Fame, or What's a Heaven For: Emily Dickinson's Teleology." *New England Quarterly* 51 (1978), 105–113.

_____. "The One and Many Emily Dickinsons." *Prairie Schooner* 51 (1978), 369–386.

Morris, Adelaide. "Two Sisters Have I." *Massachusetts Review* 22 (1981), 323–332.

Mossberg, Barbara. *Emily Dickinson: When a Writer Is a Daughter.* Bloomington: Indiana University Press, 1982.

Mudge, Jean. *Emily Dickinson and the Image of Home.* Amherst: University of Massachusetts Press, 1975.

_____. "Emily Dickinson and 'Sister Sue.' " *Prairie Schooner* 52 (1978), 90–108.

Oberhaus, Dorothy. "In Defense of Sue." *Dickinson Studies* 43 (1983), 1–25.

Odell, Ruth. *Helen Hunt Jackson.* New York: Appleton-Century, 1939.

Phillips, Elizabeth. *Emily Dickinson: Personae and Performance.* University Park: Pennsylvania State University Press, 1986.

Pollitt, Josephine. *Emily Dickinson: The Human Background of Her Poetry.* New York: Harper, 1930.

Porter, David. *Dickinson: The Modern Idiom.* Cambridge, Mass.: Harvard University Press, 1981.

St. Armand, Barton. *Emily Dickinson and Her Culture: The Soul's Society.* New York: Cambridge University Press, 1984.

———. " 'Your Prodigal': Letters of Ned Dickinson, 1879–1885." *New England Quarterly* (September 1988), 358–380.

Sewall, Richard. *The Life of Emily Dickinson.* New York: Farrar, Straus and Giroux, 1974. 2 vols.

Sherwood, William. *Circumference and Circumstance: Stages in the Mind and Art of Emily Dickinson.* New York: Columbia University Press, 1968.

Stearns, Alfred. *An Amherst Boyhood.* Amherst, Mass.: Amherst College Press, 1946.

Swenson, May. "Big My Secret, but It's Bandaged." *Parnassus* (Spring–Winter 1985), 16–44.

Taggard, Genevieve. *The Life and Mind of Emily Dickinson.* New York: Knopf, 1930.

Todd, Mabel. Diaries and journals, 1881–1895. Mabel Loomis Todd Collection, Sterling Library, Yale.

———. "Emily Dickinson's Literary Debut." *Harper's Monthly Magazine* CLX (1930), 463–471.

Todd-Dickinson lawsuit: *Supreme Judicial Court, Hampshire Co., September Law Sitting, 1898. Lavinia N. Dickinson v. Mabel Loomis Todd, et al., Defendant's Appeal* (No. 4). Same, *Plaintiff's Brief,* and *Defendant's Brief.* Mabel Loomis Todd Collection, Sterling Library, Yale.

Van Dyke, Joyce. "Inventing Emily Dickinson." *Virginia Quarterly Review* vol. 60, no. 2 (1984), 276–296.

Walsh, John. *The Hidden Life of Emily Dickinson.* New York: Simon and Schuster, 1971.

Wells, Anna. *Dear Preceptor: The Life and Times of T. W. Higginson.* Boston: Houghton Mifflin, 1963.

———. "Was Emily Dickinson Psychotic?" *American Imago* XIX (1962), 309–321.

Whicher, George. *This Was a Poet: A Critical Biography of Emily Dickinson.* New York: Scribner's, 1938.

Wolff, Cynthia. *Life of Emily Dickinson.* New York: Knopf, 1986.

Woodress, James. "Emily Dickinson." In *Fifteen American Authors Before 1900*, ed. Robert A. Rees and Earl N. Harbert. Madison: Wisconsin University Press, 1984.

Wylder, Edith. *The Last Face: Emily Dickinson's Manuscripts.* Albuquerque: New Mexico University Press, 1971.

Index